SEVENFOLD PEACE

World Peace Through
Body   Mind
Family   Community   Culture
Ecology   God

Gabriel Cousens, M.D.

H J Kramer Inc
Tiburon, California

H J Kramer Inc.
P.O. Box 1082
Tiburon, CA 94920

Library of Congress Cataloging-in-Publication Data

Cousens, Gabriel, 1943–
    Sevenfold peace: world peace through body, mind, family,
community, culture, ecology, God / Gabriel Cousens,
    p.   cm.
Includes bibliographical references.
ISBN 0-915811-28-6 (pbk.) : $4.95
    1. Peace—Religious aspects. 2. New Age movement. I. Title.
BP605.N48C68   1990
    291.1'7873—dc20   90-52704
                                                           CIP

Editor: Nancy Grimley Carleton
Cover Art and Design: Jim Marin
Typesetting: Classic Typography
Book Production: Schuettge and Carleton
Manufactured in the United States of America
This book is printed on recycled paper.

10 9 8 7 6 5 4 3 2 1

To the noble souls who are striving for peace on every level.

TO OUR READERS

The books we publish are our contribution to an emerging world based on cooperation rather than on competition, on affirmation of the human spirit rather than on self-doubt, and on the certainty that all humanity is connected. Our goal is to touch as many lives as possible with a message of hope for a better world.

Hal and Linda Kramer, Publishers

Contents

Foreword

Something is shifting in our time. As the future of life on earth is seen to be fundamentally in jeopardy, a wave of new awareness is sweeping across the planet. Everywhere people are seeing that if we continue to experience ourselves as isolated and threatened, if we continue to act as though our lives depended on conquering nature and each other, we will destroy not only ourselves but the very life-support systems that have given us birth. Everywhere there are people who are sensing the transformation that is called for if we are to continue. Everywhere there are people awakening to the possibility that life can have meaning, purpose, and pleasure when lived in accord with our deepest instincts for survival.

A spiritual instinct is arising in the collective human psyche. It is calling us out of our personal black holes, out of our hiding places and unconsciousness, and drawing us to life.

The truths of our time necessitate great changes in our ways of thinking and living. The old paradigms are giving way to ones more in keeping with the new potential to which our lives must now give expression.

As we move together into the uncharted realms of the future, few things are more important than drawing guidance from the deepest wisdom teachings of our past. For there has always lain in the human psyche the awareness of Universal Truths, and guidance to the steps involved in the so-very-human effort to bring our lives into alignment.

Gabriel Cousens's *Sevenfold Peace* is at once a guide to the steps we are asked to take, and at the same time a call to deep layers of remembrance in our beings. We are shown the way to rejoin in harmony with the rest of Creation, and to open our lives to the blessings of the Great Spirit.

It is an ancient wisdom that is drawing us into the new. *Sevenfold Peace* helps us hear the way it speaks to us personally, individually. It is a call to make our life-styles spiritual statements. It is a call to survival. Today, these have become the same task.

John Robbins
President, EarthSave
Author, *Diet for a New America*

Preface

The Essenes lived two thousand years ago, but their message is still absolutely accurate for helping us to bring peace to our planet and to ourselves.

Gabriel Cousens makes an important contribution in bringing Essene concepts to our consciousness, because peace can't come from social activism alone, from trying to change others without wanting to change ourselves. Through the example of the Essenes, he shows that peace is the result of a multidimensional approach: When we love ourself, or more exactly our selves— because we have to learn to accept all aspects of our being in order to be free of self-criticism—then we can begin to understand what peace is. A vital step to peace is to stop polluting our bodies, for the pollution of our planet is the reflection of the pollution of our bodies by an artificial nutrition.

Then, we have to learn the other aspects of peace, as Gabriel Cousens describes, so that we can be responsible human beings. It is time to step into the age of responsibility, in which "homo sapiens" becomes "homo terrestrialis" or "homo ecologicus," human beings living in harmony with all aspects of themselves and all living beings.

This book can contribute to a vital awakening. For this reason, I highly recommend it to all people who want to learn to live in peace, in joy, in health, and in creativity!

Christian Tal Schaller, M.D.

Christian Tal Schaller, M.D., is president of the "Fondation Soleil," a nonprofit organization that teaches that health can be learned. He is a pioneer in the field of health education and holistic medicine. He is an author and international lecturer, supporting many health educational centers all over the world.

Acknowledgments

I would like to express my love and gratitude to Nora Cousens, who through her love and our marriage has helped me integrate the Sevenfold Peace into my life in a real way. I also thank her for her help in editing this book. I thank Raff and Heather Cousens, my two wonderful children, for sharing their love and support and for the healthy tests they have put me through as they unfold as beautiful flowers in this Divine garden of our planet.

I remain eternally grateful to Swami Muktananda Paramahansa, whose transmission of grace and guidance in my spiritual unfoldment helped me to know the essence of peace with the Heavenly Father.

I am also indebted to Dr. Edmond Bordeaux Szekely, whose genius and Renaissance awareness have made volumes of translated books about the Essenes available to the world. He has inspired me with his clarity and depth of understanding of the Essene way of life, the Sevenfold Peace, and the Tree of Life.

I thank the following dear friends: Eliot Jay Rosen, for the days he spent proofing and editing the manuscript; Mark Mayell, for the extended time he spent making insightful suggestions about the content and form of the book; Father Dunstin Morrissey, for his suggestions and review of the manuscript with his spiritually perceptive eye; Kurt Krueger, for his feedback; and historian Raymond Brick, for his helpful insights and suggestions.

I also want to thank John Robbins for the poetic wisdom of his foreword and Tal Schaller, M.D., for his love and support in preparing this book and for his beautiful preface. My thanks also goes to Global Family, for helping me compile the resource list.

I am most grateful for the love, support, and encouragement of my publishers, Hal and Linda Kramer. I appreciate their understanding and efforts to help keep the price of this book as low as possible. I also thank Nancy Grimley Carleton for the final comprehensive editing.

Sevenfold Peace:
An Introduction

We create peace by being peace. One who is at peace brings harmony into every aspect of life. What is meant by the word peace? What are the different aspects of peace? Is peace found simply by meditating in a cave? Is peace merely the absence of war? Will we obtain peace by preventing the destruction of the rain forests, by saving the whales and dolphins, by changing our economic or political systems, or by growing and eating only organic foods? The path of Sevenfold Peace, based on the ancient teachings of the Essenes, takes us beyond narrow definitions of peace to a comprehensive and integrated understanding of the personal, social, and planetary dimensions of peace. Living this ancient, multileveled path of Sevenfold Peace lays the foundation for the establishment of lasting planetary peace. This full peace is predicated on both the inner process of personal transformation and the outer process of planetary transformation. Either by itself is not enough. **Personal and**

planetary transformation are the two wings of the dove of peace.

The Essene communities that existed in Palestine several hundred years before the time of Christ were one of the rare societies that have ever been able to create a sustainable peace on every level of their function. The seven-level path of peace that they followed was a key element in their ability to maintain peace in their community and with the surrounding communities. The Sevenfold Peace offers a modernization of ancient Essene wisdom so that we, too, can create peace in our lives and on and with the planet.

Who were the Essenes? Because they lived as a society removed from the mainstream, few historical references are found about them. The Essenes were mentioned by the Roman naturalist Pliny; the Alexandrian philosopher Philo; and the Jewish historian Josephus. Pliny the Elder, in his book *Natural History*, spoke of the Essenes as a "race by themselves, more remarkable than any in the world." Traces of Essene teachings have been found in Sumerian hieroglyphs dating back eight to ten thousand years. Some Essene symbols date from an age preceding the cataclysm that ended the Pleistocene period. The teachings of the Essenes also appear in the Zend Avesta of Zarathustra, the great Persian sage, who taught a way of life that has lasted thousands of years. The fundamental Essene teachings have been taught in ancient Persia, Egypt, and India (in the Vedas and Upanishads, and through the various yogic systems, and in Buddhism, with the sacred Bodhi Tree correlating with the Essene Tree of Life) and in Tibet, China, Palestine, and Greece (by the Pythagoreans and Stoics). Traces of Essene principles can be found in the teachings of Freemasonry, Gnosticism, the Kabbalah, and Christianity.

The Essene tradition, which perhaps was first brought to Earth by the ancient Hebrew forerunner Enoch after he was said to have ascended to heaven for thirty days and then returned to earth, is said to have reemerged with Moses' teachings of the first set of tablets brought down from Mount Sinai. In the Essene lore, according to scholar and translator of the Essene Gospel of Peace Books 1–4 Dr. Edmond Bordeaux Szekely, these esoteric teachings brought down by Moses were given to those who were spiritually ready. The second set of tablets, consisting of what we now call the Ten Commandments, comprised the exoteric teachings given to guide the vast majority, who, in their spiritual immaturity, had created the golden calf. Until now, even the relatively concrete teachings of the magnificently simple and profound Ten Commandments have been too difficult for most of the world to follow.

The Essenes taught a way of being whole and peaceful rather than a set of laws. The Essene teachings are not meant to replace the Ten Commandments, but rather to offer a way to transform oneself into the living law of the Ten Commandments. These teachings seemed to have crystallized in their clear form through the prophet Elijah on Mt. Carmel, and finally through the secret brotherhoods of the Essenes, who lived two to three centuries B.C. and during the first century A.D. The Essenes lived around the Dead Sea in Palestine and at Lake Mareotis in Egypt. The Essenes sent forth teachers from their own communities, including the Teacher of Righteousness, John the Baptist, and John the Beloved, as well as Jesus, who is said to have been raised and educated in the Essene communities. The essence of the Essene teachings can be found in the beautiful Seven Beatitudes of Jesus' Sermon on the Mount.

No one knows exactly what happened to the Essenes. In A.D. 68, forewarned of the advancing Roman legions, they hid many of their manuscripts and sacred texts, and seemed to dissolve into nonexistence. Most probably, they brought their teachings in small groups to the far corners of the earth. Many of them were said to have become Gnostics. Their knowledge has only resurfaced in this century through the finding of the Dead Sea Scrolls in 1947 at Qumran and a few manuscripts that had been preserved in monasteries. To our good fortune, some of these Essene manuscripts were found as early as 1927, in the archives of the Vatican, of the Habsburgs in Vienna, and of the British Museum, by Hungarian researcher Dr. Edmond Bordeaux Szekely, who translated them into English. Many have called Dr. Szekely the first modern Essene. Through his wise understanding and efforts, the Essene teachings have spread around the world.

The inspiration behind the commentaries for each of the seven aspects of peace described here are my own interpretations, based upon two sources: my understanding of Dr. Szekely's translations of the different Essene manuscripts and the Dead Sea Scrolls, and my direct experience practicing the Sevenfold Peace since I first began to study it in 1973. I have applied its principles to my own life in the following roles: as a married person since 1967, who now has a twenty-year-old son and seventeen-year-old daughter, and as a holistic physician, psychiatrist, certified Essene teacher and minister, leader of the Tree of Life Seminars, director of Sonoma County Peace the 21st (an international prayer and meditation for peace group), and author of *Spiritual Nutrition and the Rainbow Diet*. Because of my position as a teacher, I have also had the opportunity to learn much from seeing how others have applied these principles in their lives.

The Essene Way of Life

The Essenes practiced an agricultural, community-based life-style, away from the cities. There were no rich or poor among them because of the alignment of their economics, life-style, and society with Divine Law. The Essenes considered Divine Law to be the sum total of all the laws governing all manifestations of the forces of nature and the cosmos. This Divine Law is perhaps best summarized as the Living Law of Love and Harmony With All Creation. In accordance with their sense of Divine Law, the Essenes had no slaves and were said to be the first society to condemn slavery both in theory and practice.

Although the Essenes lived in the harsh conditions of the desert, each person's material needs, food, and shelter were easily and abundantly met because of that person's alignment with the essential harmony of the universe. The Essenes were vegetarians; they avoided any form of alcohol; and they daily fed their bodies, minds, and souls with contemplation of the earthly and cosmic forces that they poetically called angels. In the morning, they contemplated the forces (angels) of Mother Nature: Earthly Mother (ecology and nutrition), earth (topsoil), the universal life force permeating all nature, joy, sun, water, and air. In the evening, they contemplated the cosmic forces of the Heavenly Father: transcendental awareness, eternal life, creative work, peace, power to manifest God's will, love, and wisdom. At noontime, they contemplated one aspect of the Sevenfold Peace each day. These communions were a cornerstone of their society, and of their total peace and essential harmony. Through this weekly cycle, the balance and practice of peace would be reviewed each week. The results of this approach to life were extraordinary. In contrast to the short life span of the surrounding peoples, historians of the time have recorded that it was common for the Essenes to live to an average age of 120 years or more.

I present this heritage of the Sevenfold Peace as a framework for creating full peace in one's life. The Sevenfold Peace is a means for understanding how to create a holistic peace with the body, mind, family, community, culture, Earthly Mother, and Heavenly Father.

Peace in the Modern World

The holistic approach of the Sevenfold Peace often contrasts with what commonly happens among people working for a peaceful planet today. Many such people are working out of an intense, but single-issue, perspective. In the intensity of their effort, it is easy to forget, not acknowledge, or even not be aware of the other elements of the Sevenfold Peace. For example, after finishing a Tree of Life Seminar in Anchorage, Alaska, I attended the evening entertainment for a conference on bioregionalism. One of the lead speakers, who was more than a bit overweight, performed on the stage in an inebriated state. I couldn't help but contrast his keen awareness and knowledge of bioregionalism with his obvious abuse and mismanagement of the immediate bioregion of his own body. In his inebriated state, he was hardly an example of a course of action that would lead to a balanced world peace. Our talk about world peace has little meaning if we are not willing to create peace in our own immediate lives.

My own interest in the Sevenfold Peace came as a result of taking a hard look at the peace in my own life after many years of political activism. I had worked with black teen gangs on the Southside of Chicago, on school health issues while living in Central Harlem in New York City, and also on antiwar issues in San Francisco. I painfully realized that I, and most of my fellow social activists, despite our high ideals and desire for social justice, had not attained any lasting peace in our own lives. What concerned me even more was that our approaches and tactics were not particularly different from those of the opposition, only we thought we were on the "right side." We, like our opposition, were still operating on the principle that the "end justifies the means." Most of us, myself included, had been limiting ourselves with a narrow, self-righteous political focus that did not include the other six aspects

Sevenfold Peace: An Introduction   xix

of the Sevenfold Peace. This single-view focus, while effective, didn't and doesn't create the overall harmony needed for us to achieve a life of total and lasting peace on either an individual or planetary level.

After contemplating this distressing insight, I dropped all outward political activity and went inward for what turned out to be a seven-year cycle of intense meditation, prayer, fasting, and other spiritual practices. I emerged from this cycle with a grasp of the meaning of inner peace, or what some would call the transcendental peace of the Heavenly Father. I was also aware, as my political efforts had shown me, that solely focusing on the transcendental self, and how wonderfully divine it is, could lead to many imbalances. A wider perspective was needed. Intuitively, I knew I had to wait patiently for the next step of understanding and integration to appear. When I reactivated my practice of the Sevenfold Peace, the fit was perfect.

The assimilation of the Sevenfold Peace into our modern lives adds some perspective to the meaning of a fully peaceful life. Peace is not something that happens by accident. **Peace is like silence; it is always there. The lack of harmony in our lives is like noise superimposed on the silence. The issue is not how to create peace, but how to live in a way that eliminates the noise.** Dr. Robert Muller, former assistant secretary-general of the United Nations and current chancellor of the University for Peace, pointed out in an interview that past United Nations secretary-general Dag Hammarskjöld, who Dr. Muller feels became a mystic while in the United Nations, concluded "that in our time the road to sanctity went through the road of action."

Action in the world is not separate from spirituality. Peace is not something we need to run away from the world to find. It involves us as fully mature and present human beings and requires of us a full, integrated relationship to the world on every level. Past secretary-general to the United Nations U Thant added to this understanding of peace when he said, "Humans should have multiple allegiances: to oneself, to the family, to the culture, to the nation, to humanity, to the world, and to the universe." The context for these multiple allegiances was clarified by Dag Hammarskjöld before he died. He said, "We have tried to make peace by every possible means, and we have failed. We can only succeed if there is a spiritual renaissance on this planet." These multiple allegiances to peace are based on our direct, spiritual understanding of our inherent connectedness to all life as all life. The Sevenfold Peace is part of the emerging blossoming of planetary consciousness as we flower into this spiritual renaissance. It is the ancient seeding the new. So, like the lives of the Essenes of old, our lives, nurtured by the understanding of the Sevenfold Peace, can become spiritual testimonies to the total and lasting peace this world so desperately needs.

Blessed is the Child of light
Who is strong in body,
For he shall have oneness with the Earth. . . .
He who hath found peace with the body
Hath built a holy temple
Wherein may dwell forever
The spirit of God.

(Essene Gospel of Peace,
Book Two [EGP 2])

1

Peace With the Body

Peace with the body is the first level of awareness. "First shall the Son of Man seek Peace with his own body, for his body is as a mountain pond that reflects the sun when it is still and clear; but when it is full of mud and stones, it reflects nothing" (EGP 4).

There are three aspects of developing peace with the body: (1) the body as its own ecological unit; (2) the body as a planetary cell in our global organism; and (3) the cosmic body. The Essenes perceived the body as the manifestation of the laws of life and the cosmos. They studied it because they saw it as a key to the universe, following the principle "As above, so below."

Understanding the body as its own ecological unit requires an openness to what it takes to develop a healthy and harmonious body. This includes nature's seven healers, which are (1) a functionally appropriate diet for the demands of daily life and for our spiritual life (ultimately, these are the same); (2) fresh air; (3) pure water; (4) adequate sunlight; (5) exercise; (6) rest; and (7) emotional, mental, and spiritual harmony.

In our lives, we often become too busy working on our other projects to get the thirty to sixty minutes of sunlight we need per day, the pure water that once existed abundantly for all, the moderate exercise we need at least three times per week, unpolluted air outdoors, or adequate rest for our bodies. When we decide to commit ourselves to peace on every level, it is surprising how easy it is to create the time to make peace with the body. Without bringing nature's seven healers into our lives, it is difficult to discharge toxins from the body and thus the body cannot regenerate itself adequately. Consequently, our physical body slowly stops functioning in a healthy way and bodily dis-ease and disharmony begin to predominate in our system. My experience is that it usually takes about two years to establish a stable program to maintain peace with the physical body.

Peace With the Diet

Developing an appropriate diet for all aspects of our lives is a complete practice of its own. To be at peace with the diet requires both artful intelligence and trial and error. It is important to realize that the exact diet for each person needs to be individualized with regard to the amount one eats, the timing of meals, and what one eats. A first step toward developing an appropriate diet is to be clear about the purposes of the diet.

The main idea is to eat in a way that maintains and enhances the God communion in the preparation of the food, the eating of it, and the digesting of it. In my book *Spiritual Nutrition and the Rainbow Diet*, I state that the goal of eating is **"not to live to eat, or eat to live, but to eat in order to enhance one's communion with the Divine."**

A harmonious diet helps us honor, maintain, and purify the body as the physical aspect of the spirit and as the temple for the spirit in a way that keeps our minds clear and our bodies physically able to cope with the demands of our unfoldment. For example, if we eat excess sweets and throw our body out of balance into hypoglycemia, the unsteady blood sugar makes it difficult to experience sustained and deep meditations or to stay focused on a project. Blood sugar swings also contribute to periods of emotional lability, depression, or hyperirritable states. We need an appropriate diet to help us assimilate, store, and conduct the heightened cosmic energies now being generated on this planet and to enable us to handle the intensified energy released through our own spiritual development. **A diet that brings peace to our body supports us in all aspects of our lives from our physical work to our spiritual endeavors.**

A vegetarian diet is the diet most compatible with the health of the body, mind, and spirit, as well as the health of the planet. Making a slow transition to a vegetarian diet is the most peaceful way to proceed. Some achieve a vegetarian diet in two weeks; others take fifteen years. The main idea is to start. From the perspective of the Sevenfold Peace, a harmonious process is more important than how quickly the goal is reached. Some people start by eliminating red meat from their diet, then chicken and fish. Others start by observing one vegetarian day per week and increase the numbers of days until they get up to seven days per week. It is important to be gentle with yourself in making this change.

A vegetarian diet that consists of about eighty percent raw foods and twenty percent cooked foods adequately supports peace with the body. In my experience and according to some of the great nutritional teachers such as Paavo Airola, Ph.D., Victoras Kulvinskas, M.S., and Dr. Edmond Szekely, this combination is generally the healthiest for optimal bodily function. The diet should include high-energy foods such as sprouts and freshly picked fruits and vegetables, some nuts and seeds, and, of course, grains and legumes.

To help us let go of the inaccurate and fearful thought forms that cause resistance to a vegetarian diet, we need to recognize that the statistics from around the world overwhelmingly show that a vegetarian diet is far superior to a meat-eating diet in terms of immediate health benefits and effects on longevity and physical endurance. As far back as 1917, research published in the *Yale Medical Journal* by Professor Irving Fisher showed that vegetarians have about twice the endurance of meat eaters. In 1961, the *Journal of the American Medical Association* editorialized, "A vegetarian diet can prevent ninety-seven percent of our coronary occlusions." In *Diet for a New America*, John Robbins points out that vegetarians who don't consume dairy products (vegans) have one-tenth as many heart attacks as meat eaters between the critical ages of forty-five to sixty-five. Vegetarians are even found to have fewer cases of anemia than meat eaters. The *American Journal of Clinical Nutrition* reported in its March 1983 issue that vegetarian women had less than one-half the instance of osteoporosis of meat-eating men. Researchers at leading research institutions such as Harvard and even the U.S. Department of Agriculture Survey on American Vegetarians have conceded that a vegetarian diet in advanced industrial areas such as the United States and Western Europe supplies more than adequate protein and meets all basic nutritional needs.

Peace With the Global Body

Most foods that are healthful for our individual bodies also seem to bring us into a peaceful relationship with ourselves as part of the planetary ecological body. Peace on one level often begets peace on another level. For example, a diet that doesn't require killing cattle, goats, sheep, chickens, turkeys, birds, or fish brings us into harmony with nature's universal law of love. A vegetarian is no longer directly participating in the creation of the suffering, pain, and death of animals on this planet. In the words of Jesus as recorded in the Essene Gospel of Peace, Book One, "Kill neither men, nor beasts, nor yet the food which goes into your mouth. For if you eat living food, the same will quicken you, but if you kill your food, the dead food will kill you also." Many have made the point that the attitude that allows us to kill animals for fun and food is the same attitude that helps to create war. Thomas Tyron (1634–1703), a concerned Quaker, warned his people that the violence of killing animals for food stemmed from the same source of "wrath" as the killing of humans. He predicted that many of his Quaker brethren in Pennsylvania who were not vegetarians would eventually take up arms for war, and he was proven correct. The violence of killing animals for our dinner table rests upon the same foundation of "justifiable" violence that often leads to killing people.

As we begin to expand our understanding of peace with the diet and body to other levels, we see that it also links us with the planetary ecological organism. A fully peaceful diet regularly honors our food as the main interface between ourselves and nature and brings us into harmony with nature and its universal laws. It establishes us in harmony with the ecological issues of food and peace on our planet. What we eat directly affects the problems of world hunger and global ecology. In the book *Diet for a New America,* author and social activist John Robbins links the following startling facts to a meat-eating diet: Sixty million people starve to death each year; our rain forests and other forests around the world are turning to deserts at an alarming rate, precipitating the greenhouse effect; four million acres of topsoil are lost each year in the United States alone; much of our water is polluted; and we are moving toward a shortage of clean water.

Raising animals for the meat and dairy products at our dinner table has a significant effect on our ecological system. It accounts for about eighty-five percent of the topsoil loss, and it consumes about one-half of the total water used in the United States. Livestock produce twenty times the excrement as the human population of the United States. Livestock in the United States regularly eat enough grain and soy to feed the U.S. population five times over. The total world livestock regularly eat about twice the calories as the human world population receives. It is ecologically shocking to realize (as pointed out by author Frances Moore Lappé in her revised edition of *Diet for a Small Planet*) that meat eaters require four thousand gallons of water per day and three and one-half acres per year to produce the meat and dairy products they consume. Vegans, or those who do not eat meat or dairy products, require one-sixth of an acre of land per year and three hundred gallons of water per day to supply their food. In other words, **approximately twenty vegans can live off the same land and water supply required to sustain one meat eater.** Someone who doesn't eat dairy products or meat saves one acre of trees per year because of the smaller quantity of resources this diet demands. On our planet, with its ever-increasing shortages of land and water, this is a significant difference. The famous nutritionist Jean Mayer, in a U.S. Senate Select Committee hearing in 1977, reported that if meat eaters were to cut their annual meat consumption by ten percent, the sixty million people who starve to death each year could have adequate food. This doesn't mean that those who are starving would get the food. As Frances Moore Lappé, author of *Diet for a Small Planet* and leader of the antihunger organization Food First, points out, the basic cause of hunger today is a "scarcity of justice, not a scarcity of food." Hunger is a social disease.

As much as some of us would like to ignore it, what we eat affects the planetary organism. Although many of us have worked effectively for the survival of the earth, adopting a vegetarian diet eliminates the level of contradiction between how we live and what we do beyond our personal lives to save the planet. Presently, according to the April 1990 *Vegetarian Times*, 76 percent of the United States population supports ecological action to save the planet, but only 2.8 percent are vegetarians. Sister Elizabeth Seton summarized our task nicely: "Live simply so that others may simply live." **Because a vegetarian diet brings peace with the individual body and the planetary body, it is part of the blueprint for a peaceful planet.**

Peace With the Cosmic Body

On a cosmic level, the body is the vehicle we are given through which our thoughts, emotions, and feelings of love arise and take expression as a manifestation of Divine Will on earth. In terms of full spiritual development, honoring the body not only as the temple of the spirit but as the manifestation of the spirit leads us to what some call "full body enlightenment." Peace with the body leads us into the nowness of the physical state. The experience of peace with the body can be described as the awareness of a sense of full and delightful presence in the body. We spontaneously begin to have conscious contact with the energetic planes of our physical existence. When the body is in harmony, the subtle energetic flow of the cosmos can be felt moving through us in an exquisite, radiant, quiet ecstasy.

To be fully at peace with the body necessitates a perspective that we are not our body, that our body is a reflection of who we ultimately are on the spiritual level. This viewpoint motivates us to take appropriate care of our physical instrument, but not to fixate our ego on it. To know we are not the body helps us overcome our primal fear of death. Fear of death, ultimately the source of all fears, comes from our mistaken identification with our body. When the fear of death diminishes, then we can be completely at peace in our body. When fear fades, peace and love flourish.

Developing an appropriate way of life and diet in the context of an overall peaceful way of life aligns us with a greater planetary harmony. For our body to become a full manifestation of the spirit on this planet takes some time. During this transition, it is important to be at peace with and tolerant of the body, rather than forcing changes too quickly. This allows the transition to be made in a harmonious and peaceful way. With persistence and patience, most life-style and dietary changes can be made comfortably in the course of one or two years.

The crown of wisdom makes peace and
    perfect health to flourish. *(EGP 2)*

When this power [of thought] is guided by
    holy wisdom,
Then the thoughts of the Son of Man lead
    him to the heavenly kingdoms
And thus is paradise built on earth;
Then it is that your thoughts uplift the
    souls of men,
As the cold water of a rushing stream
    revives your body in the summer heat.
                                  (EGP 4)

2

Peace With the Mind

Peace with the mind involves creating a peaceful mind on three levels: the individual mind, or the totality of an individual's thoughts; the planetary mind, which is the totality of all the thoughts of all the individuals on the planet; and the cosmic mind, which is the totality of all of the cosmic thoughts in the universe.

Many people in our modern world suffer from a mind at war with itself. It is my observation, and that of the Essenes, that the mind tends to move toward a more peaceful state when we bring our life-style into harmony with the unwritten laws that govern the universe and the basic laws of human conduct. These laws can be found in the teachings of all the great scriptures. Love your neighbor as your Divine Self is a simple summary of the laws for human interaction.

Peace With the Individual Mind

Much of our lack of peace is the result of willingly exploiting ourselves by creating an overextended, imbalanced life-style that is organized around trying to accumulate what we often do not need, which is usually detrimental to our physical, emotional, mental, and spiritual well-being. This self-exploitation happens when we become ruled by our desires rather than being in control of our desires. The result of this disharmonious state is that we lose touch with the very same peace, love, and tranquility that we hope to attain by fulfilling our worldly desires. The Essene Teacher of Righteousness in the Essene Gospel of Peace, Book Four, explains it beautifully: **"Do ye not, then, barter that which is eternal for that which dieth in an hour."** Chinese philosopher Lao-tzu discusses another aspect of this human issue succinctly: "Without desire there is tranquility, and in this way all things would be at Peace."

My experience, and that of many teachers from time immemorial, is that the primary method of controlling and dissolving the desires of the mind has been the practice of meditation on the Divine. Meditation eventually dissolves the desires of the mind that usurp our birthright of tranquility and peace. Prayer and a variety of other methods can also work. Meditation has the power to bring us in touch with the supreme nectar of the Eternal. It is through the experience of this Divine Communion that we are filled with enough contentment, insight, and power not to be controlled by our desires. The experience of Divine Communion puts us in touch with a sublime, noncausal joy (joy that comes without one's having to do something specific to create it) that naturally fills us with such peace that the goal of all our desires, which is peace and contentment, is spontaneously fulfilled. It is not that desires never arise again, but that we are no longer controlled by them because with meditation we can go right to the ultimate goal of all desires. In this state, one can serve humanity without a lot of mental confusion.

Meditation can create a perspective that also helps us get in touch with who we are and the best way to fulfill our life purpose on this planet. When the mind is clear, we are also better able to direct the currents of emotion and bodily activities that move through us. Another result of meditation that brings peace with the mind is the direct realization that we are not our thoughts, or even our mind. It is possible to experience directly that we are the awareness that is beyond the mind. In this way, we develop an ability to witness our thoughts rather than become controlled by them.

Through meditation, or other ways of working with the mind, we are also able to understand that the world is how we perceive it to be. If we perceive it through a filter of negative thoughts, we tend to respond more often to the environment in a negative way and thus amplify negative thoughts and experiences. Conversely, if we see the world through the understanding of the ancient wisdom that whatever God does is for the best, the same events are transformed into positive occurrences. After enough meditation, one develops the conscious power to choose naturally to see the glass "half full" rather than "half empty."

Another source of mental unrest arises when we do not live in accordance with what we believe in our hearts. To continue to act contrary to our beliefs, and not live and work in ways that we know will elevate us, slowly robs us of our life essence and diminishes the meaningfulness of our lives. Living a life of quiet desperation does not bring peace of mind. I am always impressed by the joy in people's hearts when they let go of what they think they need and begin to live in accordance with their own right livelihood and as the brightest lights they can manifest.

Peace With the Planetary Mind

Understanding the planetary mind, which is the sum of all the thoughts of humanity, is a key to understanding the thought form for peace movement. All of our thoughts spontaneously add themselves to the planetary mind. Each individual's mind is affected by the planetary mind, so what we contribute to the planetary mind, positively or negatively, affects each one of us on this planet. The Essenes recognized thought as one of the most powerful forces on the planet. By taking responsibility for creating positive thoughts, all of us, as individuals and even more so as groups of individuals, can elevate the consciousness on the planet. Researchers such as Dr. Tiller, head of material sciences at Stanford University, have hypothesized that the power of the group thought form is equal to the square of the number of people in the group. This is supported by the understanding from Leviticus 26:7–8 that "one hundred will chase away ten thousand." Since 1973, many studies have demonstrated that when a critical number of meditators gather together to focus on the highest truth there is a statistical decrease in the amount of social disorder in the area in which they are meditating. The research cited by authors Elaine and Arthur Aron in *The Maharishi Effect* points to a critical number to bring about this social effect, which seems to be around one percent or the square root of one percent of a population area. Perhaps the variance depends on the degree of intensity of the meditators.

The profound implications of this phenomenon is one of the greatest hopes we have for world peace. The proven power of group meditations has been a source of growth of thought form for peace movements such as Peace the 21st, which encourages peacemakers to meditate for peace on each equinox and solstice; World Healing Hour, whose supporters meditate for peace at noon Greenwich time on December 31st of each year; and a variety of other groups that suggest we meditate collectively for peace at 7:00 A.M. or noon daily, at noon on Sundays, or on the last day of each month. To practice this principle actively is a wonderful way to participate in creating peace consciousness on the planet. It is a way of healing the soul of the planet.

People's thoughts form a force field around them that both transmits thought forms to the planetary mind and receives thought forms from the planetary mind. We thus live, move, think, feel, and act in the planetary thought field. In a very concrete way, we are affected by the planetary mind whenever we turn on the TV, read the newspaper, or watch a movie. Can we dispute that the Beatles, the *Star Wars* films, the "Star Trek" series, or even Shirley MacLaine's TV series have had an effect on planetary consciousness? We are just beginning to recognize the impact of seeing people killed, shot, and tortured in our own living rooms on television. According to George Gerbner, a communications professor at the University of Pennsylvania and coauthor of the study "Violence Profile 1967–1989: Enduring Patterns," seventy percent of prime-time network programs use violence, and ninety percent of programs are violent during children's hours. Advertisements including violence during children's programming have increased to twenty-five acts of violence per hour. The average American has seen eighteen thousand murders before graduating from high school. According to an Associated Press article of April 16, 1990, the American Academy of Pediatrics at its 1990 convention said that "long-term television viewing is one cause of violent and aggressive behavior in children."

The violent thought forms reflected in the media cannot help but increase the violence in our society. Peter Russell's concept of the global brain, which states that global mass communication will grow as complex and cross-connected as the human brain itself by the year 2000, further supports the idea that the creation of a tangible planetary mind is taking place.

The key question is, what is being communicated by this planetary mind? By creating thoughts of a high vibration, we automatically help protect ourselves and others from the lower vibratory thoughts of war, hate, jealousy, wasteful living, excessive desire for wealth, and so forth. It has been my observation that by a steady practice of meditation, balanced living in harmony with the universal and natural laws, and a supportive social and spiritual system, we become increasingly immune to the negative thought-form forces that are being generated all over this planet. By adding thoughts of peace, we help to shift the planetary mind toward peace. The good news is that we do not need a majority to shift the planetary mind toward peace; it may take just one percent of our population.

Peace With the Cosmic Mind

We connect with the cosmic mind when we are creating and living in harmony with the highest thoughts. The more we work in harmony with the cosmic mind and experience its manifestations in our surroundings and in our every cell, the more we are transformed. The more we live this way, the more we become one with the cosmic mind. Often we start with a fleeting seed experience of the harmony of the cosmic mind, and with work it grows into an ever-increasing steady state. By becoming conscious of the Law and choosing to act in harmony with it, we become co-creators. The power to act at one with the Divine Will comes through freeing ourselves from all our ego attachments. We then become more aware of our present and past disharmonies and restructure our thoughts and belief system to correct these disharmonies.

If we remain unconscious of our disharmonious thoughts or choose not to bring them into harmony, it becomes much easier to be affected by the overwhelming disharmony of the current planetary mind field. By accepting disharmonious thoughts into our lives, we simultaneously create an imbalance in our system. By a principle similar to harmonic resonance, any disharmonious thought we accept alters our own mental body in a way that sends out a frequency that attracts other similar disharmonious thoughts. So from one imbalanced thought we end up attracting a whole disharmonious force into our system. This disharmonious force then acts on the emotional body, causing imbalance on the emotional level. When both the mental and emotional bodies are out of harmony, we find that the physical body in turn takes on this disharmony as physical dis-ease. These disharmonies then make a discordant physical, emotional, and mental planetary force around the person, which then affects the physical, emotional, and mental bodies of everyone else on the planet. Those closest to us are usually the most affected. This planetary imbalance may then affect other planetary worlds. It is amazing how one negative, limiting, or disharmonious thought can cause such a mess. Like an uncontrolled mob, a disharmonious thought can become as contagious as a virulent virus. The good news is that a harmonious thought sets off a chain reaction toward harmony, by attracting all the resonant harmonious thoughts in the universe. This is the principle upon which the thought form for peace meditation works.

How can we make sure our thoughts are harmonious so that we don't create a cosmic mess? One key secret to maintaining harmonious thoughts is to **start every thought with love. Love as the source of the first thought and word will shape the following thoughts,**

words, and actions. Although there are a variety of ways to maintain this love consciousness, I have found that meditation is the most powerful; prayer, good fellowship, and selfless service also work. In meditation, we are able to go to the direct experience of love. By meditating regularly, we constantly reinforce this love awareness.

From the place of love, we create a thought form of harmony that brings us into complete cooperation with the Divine Law. Through complete cooperation with the cosmic law, peace and harmony can be brought to the planet. Peace through material, economic, or other technical approaches has not been, and will never be, enough to bring lasting peace to this planet. These left-brain technologies, however, may provide great service to humanity if practiced in harmony with the cosmic law and powered by love.

Let thy love be as a sun
Which shines on all the creatures of the
    earth,
And does not favor one blade of grass
For another.
And this love shall flow as a fountain
From brother to brother. . . .
He who hath found peace with his brothers
Hath entered the kingdom of Love. *(EGP 2)*

3

Peace With the Family

Peace with the family operates on personal, planetary, and cosmic levels. It refers to harmony with the emotional or feeling body. Peace with the family refers to harmonious day-to-day relationships with our immediate family, relatives, friends, and associates. When we have peace with our own body and mind, then we have peace with ourselves. We are thus able to interact with our family and immediate social environment with unconditional love. To love ourselves unconditionally gives us the strength to love others unconditionally, and thus fulfill the teaching to love our neighbor as ourselves.

Just as the individual thought body is the combination of all our thoughts, so the individual feeling body is the cumulative field of all our individual emotions. There is also a planetary atmosphere created by the summation of all the individual feeling bodies on the planet. Every emotion we create sets up a resonance with similar feelings in the planetary feeling body. Since the healthy function of the feeling body is to express love, when we are in balance we give off feelings of love that increase the love resonance of the planetary feeling body.

Unfortunately, the opposite occurs when we create a disharmonious feeling. By virtue of the resonant field of the disharmonious feeling, we tune in to the force of all similar disharmonious feelings and attract that energy to ourselves. This destructive force not only amplifies our individual negative feelings, but also directly affects the functioning of our physical bodies. There is a new field developing called psychoendocrinology that has produced research showing how our emotional state affects the immune system. For example, when people are psychologically depressed, the evidence shows that their immune systems also become depressed. As Norman Cousins's laughter therapy illustrates, the opposite is also true. A happy emotional state encourages a strong immune system. According to Dr. Szekely, the Essenes believed that allowing the feeling body to fulfill its true function, which is to express love, is the most powerful tool for creating health and joy.

At one point in the historical evolution of the human race and, analogously, in our individual evolution starting from infancy, the instinctual and feeling body dominated our interactions. To be ruled by our emotions does not bring peace. It may even lead to a habitually reactive way of dealing with the world rather than an interactive way. Mob psychology is the extreme example of this. In the peace process, we make the transition toward creating a mature synthesis of our physical, feeling, and thought bodies. Our wisdom mind is given the power to focalize our emotions and bring harmony and integration for all three bodies. This doesn't mean that we aren't in touch with the full range of our feelings. It means that our actions on a personal and planetary level are not simply an acting out of our primitive or impulsive emotions or desires. The Peace Pilgrim, a woman who walked across this country for decades spreading the message of peace, put it nicely when she said, **"If we were mature people, war would be no problem; it would be impossible."** To be mature, from the point of view of peace, means to live with an awareness of love and tolerance, which harmonizes with the wisdom of our intellect.

In this context, suffering is caused by desiring anything other than God. When we extend this principle of the personal ego desire/suffering cycle, we can see how a collective attachment on a national level may lead to a blind nationalism, which in turn leads us into war in order to satisfy a national ego. This sort of uncontrolled national emotional body has created much planetary suffering throughout history.

Families exist not only for propagation, but also to provide a training ground for learning how to develop intimacy. This function is true for all long-term relationships. Life in the family is designed by its very nature to help our feeling body mature. Being able to love without manipulation is required if we are to have peace with the feeling body. In true intimate relationships, one experiences durable love, steady trust, and a willingness to be vulnerable. **Durable intimacy requires** a continual willingness to suffer a wound of the heart without contracting the heart in fear and rejection. This is the key to developing a loving relationship. When we have developed a mature feeling body, we are able to love without controlling or being controlled. We are able to love out of choice and not need. This is not "love as a business deal," which involves subtle levels of codependency such as "You love me, and I love you" or "You give me what I want, and I give you what you want." Mature love means loving without slipping into a state of feeling betrayed, rejected, or unloved if we feel our requirements for love are not met. Fear, hate, revenge, a state of unlove, feelings of "You don't love me," and other aspects of a closed heart create disharmony in the feeling body. **The most direct way to know love in every moment is to be love in every moment rather than to demand it from someone else.** One of the teachings of peace with the family is that fundamental love cannot be demanded.

For most people, the ability to be love in every moment comes from creating a constant communion with the Divine One, the One who is ever present on all levels of our existence. Those of us who choose to take the risk of nonmanipulative, open-hearted love draw love spontaneously to ourselves. Those of us who are constantly searching for love usually do not find it until we, ourselves, become immersed in love. **Love does not stop when we are rejected or seemingly not loved; it stops when we withhold love from another or forget our connection with the Divine.**

If our dear ones temporarily try to punish us with rejection and a withdrawal of love, we must learn to

overcome the automatic ego desire to react by reject-
ing them and withdrawing our love. This is one of the
hardest practices of peace with the family. It means,
for example, that as parents we do not succumb to the
temporary urge to close our hearts when our teenage
children go through their rejection rituals aimed at
making us feel unloved, unneeded, and unappreciated.
My experience, as a parent of two teens, has been that
an open, although sometimes wounded, heart eventually wins over teenagers' love because it preserves
their sense of being loved. When a teen can't create
rejection in us, love remains.

Since 1967, my marriage relationship has been a
great source of spiritual growth because both of us
continue to challenge each other in the context of con-
sciously maintaining open-hearted vulnerability. This
is a powerful practice. Through the experience of an
ever-blossoming marriage and in my work as a family
therapist, I have found that when people have the
courage to love each other in full, vulnerable intimacy,
without holding resentments, their relationship will
work out to its highest potential. **Love in the family
brings peace.** It turns us into velveteen rabbits. *The Velveteen Rabbit* is a story by Margery Williams about a toy
rabbit who became a real rabbit through his unrelent-
ing love of a little boy. No matter if his hair was worn
thin, his button eye hanging on a thread, or he was
thrown in the garbage by the boy's mother, the velveteen rabbit's love persisted. He understands that real
is not how you are made; it's a thing that happens to
you when a child loves you for a long time.

The ability to feel the wound of love without retaliation creates peace in all sorts of human interactions. Recently I was presenting some peace proposals at a school board meeting, and I was bitterly and personally attacked by a religious antipeace group for being "a meditator, a New Age leader, and for promoting peace in the schools." After the meeting, I wrote a letter to one of the people who had attacked me. I told her that the only way I could deal with the nature of her attack was to forgive her completely. She responded beautifully, and we were able to establish a friendly and respectful dialogue. This reinforced for me the meaning of the words of Jesus, "Love thy enemies." The truth is that loving our enemies means we have no enemies; love turns them all into friends. To love and forgive in this way is a wonderful practice that brings peace to every aspect of family and community life, and it is the bedrock for creating a world family. **The way of Peace is the way of love. Forgiveness is the way of love.**

Behind the effort of loving fully is the inspiration of Divine Love, which is both the result and the cause of the ability and courage to love. Communion with the Divine sustains us in the state of harmony and love with our family. Love of the Divine is the ultimate source of a harmonious feeling body and peace with the family.

When there is peace with the family, when we have achieved some degree of love for ourselves and love for those in close relationship with us, then it seems almost natural that we begin to move toward peace with humanity. In England in the 1930s, a unique ten-year study on what contributes to health was carried out at the Pioneer Health Centre; it was called the Peckham Experiment (described in detail in *The Peckham*

26   Sevenfold Peace

Experiment by Innes Pearse and Lucy Crocker). It involved over five thousand families. This study found that the unit of health was not the individual, but the family. In addition, when the health of the family was in jeopardy, the individuals tended to withdraw from social engagement outside the family. When the family health was strong, then the individual members would participate more actively in the world outside of the family. Loving family relationships are an important template for how we function in the world community. The great Chinese sage Lao-tzu put it nicely, **"The wise accept all people as their own family."**

The belief that we are all one family is not simply a New Age idea. Its roots can be traced back at least as far as the Old Testament, with the Hebrew tribe's belief that peace between people is one of the foundations of creation. According to the commentary of *The Torah Anthology* (published in 1730 by one of the great sages of the time, Rabbi Yakaav Culi), the Hebrews were referred to in the plural in the Old Testament until they received the divine guidance of the Torah on Mt. Sinai. Once they were spiritually unified through the Torah, the Old Testament then refers to them in the singular. When they lived in unity, they were considered as a single soul. Lasting peace on this planet will come when we experience all the people of the world as one soul.

There shall be no peace among peoples
Till there be one garden of the brotherhood
Over the earth. *(EGP 2)*

4

Peace With Humanity

Peace with humanity is the ultimate result of a shift in individual consciousness to the awareness of global unity. To accomplish this, we must break our habitual identification with what Alan Watts called being "skin-encapsulated" entities who see everyone outside of our own skin as different, separate, and foreign. This fractionalized, alienated attitude of perceiving ourselves as separate from the whole may be healed by seeing ourselves as part of the whole. The more we meditate and try to live in harmony with natural and Divine laws, the more we are likely to experience this oneness.

In *The Global Brain*, Peter Russell hypothesizes that the escalating pace of planetary communication is resulting in an ever-increasing shared awareness of international interconnectedness. For the first time in history, we are able to use this planetary communication to have regular, simultaneous global peace meditations, such as Peace the 21st and the World Healing Hour on December 31st, as well as the Concert for Bangladesh and Live-Aid. For the first time in history, almost all of the planet has direct access to spiritual teaching from past to present. Because of the ease of international transportation, general international turmoil, international corporate activity, and the psychospiritual interface of East and West, we are beginning to experience the world as smaller and more unified. We still have a long way to go in this transition to a full sense of global unity, and a corresponding absence of an "us and them" mentality. But this will surely happen as the global brain process unfolds. One of our roles as peacemakers is to help give birth to this evolutionary step.

The full synchrony of planetary harmony can't really be understood by the intellect alone; it is more of an intuitive experience. The intellect can talk of it, but to experience it directly and live it in our daily lives requires a deeper and more direct approach. This is one area where the meditative experience, in which we naturally and spontaneously experience this unity awareness, is a most effective way to imbibe this consciousness. **Meditation in this context is not a luxury, but a necessity for global survival.**

Peace with humanity is harmony between groups of people on a social, economic, political, and spiritual basis. It is the culmination of the collective process of individuals who are at peace with themselves and have shifted into unity consciousness.

Humanity has never experienced full peace in any age in history because there have not been enough mature individuals who were willing and able to live according to natural law and Divine law. The rich and strong have almost always exploited the poor and weak, economically, socially, religiously, and politically. Great wealth is concentrated in the hands of a few. The poor perennially struggle to regain some of this wealth, often just to survive. Unfortunately, both the suppressor and the suppressed are forced into disharmony. According to Raimon Panikkar while professor of religious studies at the University of California at Santa Barbara, in a theoretical global village of one hundred families, ninety do not speak English, sixty-five can't read, eighty have never flown in an airplane, seventy have no drinking water at home, seven families own sixty percent of the village and consume eighty percent of its energy, and only one family has a university education.

In our world today, sixty million people die of starvation each year according to statistics from the Institute for Food and Development Policy, and approximately fourteen and a half million of them are children. We have more pounds of ammunition per person than we do of food (according to Doug Mattern, the secretary-general of the World Citizen Assembly). We spend $16,500 per soldier in the world and $260 per child for education. Sources compiled by Greenpeace show that in 1988, in the United States, the richest part of the global village, one percent of the population owns thirty-six percent of the wealth. The U.S. ranks last among leading industrialized nations in economic fairness as defined by the proportion of the income going to the top twenty percent of the population versus that going to the bottom twenty percent. With this much disparity in the distribution of basic resources, we do not have to look far to find the economic causes of war or to understand that starvation is a social disorder.

The Essenes taught that this sort of social imbalance comes from disharmony in our personal lives, which then manifests on social and political levels. They felt that both poverty and riches were a result of deviation from the law. The Essenes, although living simply, always had excess food to share with, and personal time for service in, the surrounding communities. One of their great messages that is relevant for our modern world is that **if we live by the Divine and natural laws we will all experience abundance.**

A Peaceful Economy

Our modern economic thinking has some of its roots in the philosophy of Francis Bacon (1561–1626) and Thomas Hobbes (1588–1679), who believed that nature is a limitless resource to be exploited to meet humanity's personal needs. In their anthropomorphic ego-centered approach, Bacon and Hobbes believed that wealth could be defined as power over other people. In this context, they saw human life as an unending competitive struggle for power. Adam Smith (1723–1790), in his classic book *The Wealth of Nations*, has often been quoted out of context to support this position of pure *laissez-faire*. Robert Nisbet, Albert Schweitzer Professor of Humanities Emeritus at Columbia University in New York, in his book *History of the Idea for Progress*, points out that, contrary to the current historical mythology, Adam Smith was deeply sensitive to the needs of the poor and the working class. Although he was in favor of competition and free enterprise, he always tempered this view with the qualification that people observe the rule of justice. The current capitalist economists have consistently omitted *the rule of justice* aspect in their citations of Adam Smith to validate their amoral approach to economic thinking. The present situation of worldwide hunger, poverty, and economic disharmony in our global village are ample evidence that this approach has not worked for the benefit of humanity or the planet. The economics of peaceful abundance, which the Essenes successfully demonstrated in their communities, was based on an economic justice for everyone.

Why is there so much poverty, injustice, and environmental degradation on the same planet where there is so much abundance and unparalleled riches? A significant reason is that our world economic system is not connected to a planetary morality. As soon as we take economics away from considerations of world peace, prosperity, and service to the whole, and toward the pursuit of personal self-interest, we have sown the breeding grounds of social disorder. Without peace as a consideration in economic decisions, we lack the clarity to make a distinction between useful production and services, such as day-care, affordable housing, and health care, and those areas of economic productivity that are harmful to humanity, such as the armaments industry, the junk food industry, or the tobacco industry. It is a national disgrace, for example, that as the evidence is rising that cigarettes contribute to lung cancer, respiratory diseases, and cardiovascular diseases, we find our tobacco companies actively trying to get people in Third World countries to take up smoking. There are even some rock concerts in the Third World where an empty pack of cigarettes of a particular brand is enough for admission. **Economics without morality brings chaos, not peace. For economics to aid in the creation of world peace, it must be organized in the service of world peace.**

Conventional economics is presently in conflict not only with social needs, but with ecological, spiritual, and commonsense needs. In conventional economics, our decisions to exploit natural resources are based on the crudest measure, the price of the commodity on the world market. The more obvious results of this policy are seen in worldwide poverty, in millions of acres of fertile topsoil becoming desert, and in the greenhouse effect resulting from the destruction of the rain forests. In 1987, the World Commission on Environment and Development published a report entitled "Our Common Future." The commission stated, "Economics and ecology must be completely integrated in decision-making and law-making processes, not just to protect the environment, but also to protect and promote development" (*Greenpeace* magazine, January–February 1989). As economist Herman Daly once said, **"There is something fundamentally wrong in treating the earth as if it were a business in liquidation."**

Humanity is not in good health; it is being eaten away by the cancer of personal, national, and international separateness. We are still choosing to work only for the ego-centered self, family, or nation. We still seek to take wealth from those we consider outside of us, in whatever way we can. How do we overcome the fear-based greed and the thirst for power and domination that bring so much world disharmony? Through meditation and prayer we are able to go beyond ego-based fear to the direct experience of love and unity. **In the condition of harmony, it is fine to seek riches because we are ready to seek them where they really are, in the gold of God Communion.** This gold is not the gross form of light that has condensed to physical gold but light as it exists in its primary form. To become rich with this light brings us to the real wealth of peace, love, and joy. Those who take in this light condense it within themselves to become the gold of awareness. We become so rich in this gold of awareness that we actually want to share our wealth with others. To realize where the real riches are and what they are is the key to all levels of personal, familial, national, and international peace.

When enough people experience the golden light of consciousness, international exploitation will be transformed into a new era of economic and social harmony. Then international exploitation will cease on the most fundamental level because we will have learned to keep what is necessary for our material well-being, in a consciousness of abundant simplicity, and to share the rest with our brothers and sisters throughout the world. Our economics will be in the service of peace.

The study of our own body function will give us some clues about peace with humanity. How is it that the cells of our body have organized themselves in such a way that they work efficiently and harmoniously with one another to create a healthy body? As the human race, are we so out of control that we cannot do the same? As individuals, we can be likened to the individual cells that make up the human body, just as we make up the planetary human body, and if we could mimic the harmony of our cells as a planetary body, we would all enjoy health, love, and prosperity. **In our body, only a cancer cell acts, as we humans do in the world body, separately, disharmoniously, and as a foreigner to the body.** The natural and divine laws are played out in the microcosm of our cellular and bodily function as well as in the macrocosm of the world and universe. If we were committed enough to peace to follow these inherent laws on every level of our life, planetary peace would be a real possibility.

Respect for International Law

Our institutions reflect our belief systems, and some good progress is being made in the external world as there is a sense of an increasing shift toward a global awareness. Supporting institutions like the United Nations and the World Court is helpful because they are the first steps on a social and political level for creating world peace. The external laws, policies, and efforts at international justice of these institutions support and create an international matrix needed for a shift toward international brother- and sisterhood. Perhaps, as part of this movement toward strengthening international institutions, we are now in the process of a paradigm shift toward respect for civil and human rights as a value system to guide us to work out differences in the world community rather than the old mode of seeing war as a way to solve problems.

There is often some public resistance to a shift toward legal, economic, and political cooperation with a larger social unit. Many people are afraid of change. The process of expanding our experience of community from smaller social units to larger units, such as in the transition from family to tribe, village to county, county to state, state to nation, and, finally, a planetary shift of individual nations to a global United Nations, encounters the same type of fear and resistance at each step. People fear that by expanding to a larger unit they will lose their control over the smaller unit. They fear that expanding their experience of community will weaken their existing unit. Some become afraid that a step toward a higher level of world order will detract from the present family, state, and national unity. What they do not understand is that by creating peace and cooperation with the larger unit the survival and functioning of the smaller unit is enhanced.

These limiting concepts of patriotism are not new to any country, including the United States. If we go back in time to the creation of the United States, a similar struggle took place in moving from a loose confederation of thirteen colonies to the formation of the United States. During postrevolutionary days, George Washington tried to persuade his New Jersey troops to swear allegiance to the United States. They refused, because they felt that New Jersey was their country. The sentiment against a United States of America was so strong that immediately after the revolution there was no national government, only thirteen sovereign colonies. In 1777, representatives of the colonies got together to create the Articles of Confederation and Perpetual Union. It took five years for the article to be ratified. Under the Confederation, there was no executive leader and the Continental Congress did not have the power to make enforceable laws. No court system existed to settle disputes. Because each of the thirteen colonies could break the agreements without penalty, the Confederation began to fall apart. Trade between colonies was curtailed, and greed and political quackery took over. No one really benefited. Currency was devalued from one state to another, so that a man traveling south from New Hampshire with $100 had only $20.24 when he reached Georgia, even if he had spent nothing on the journey. In Pennsylvania and Delaware, there was religious freedom. In Massachusetts, Catholic priests could be imprisoned for life. And in Rhode Island, Catholics could not vote.

Because the Confederation allowed a social chaos that benefited only a few and penalized the vast majority, a constitutional convention was called in 1787. The delegates had to work out a system that neither governed too much, creating another kingship, nor governed too little, allowing anarchy to reign. There was much resistance because of many of the fears I described earlier. Some of the delegates were staunchly anti-Federalist; others called Federalism naive, idealistic, and premature. But three months after the convention, Delaware was the first state to ratify the new constitution of the United States. It took nine months before the minimum number of nine states needed to bring the U.S. constitution into existence had signed. Some states, such as Rhode Island, took as long as three years to ratify, and then by only two votes. Today, it is easy to look back and understand the great benefit of unifying the individual colonies into the United States on legal, economic, and political levels. On an international level, we are now at a similar juncture to the one the colonies faced in 1787. It is now time to expand the vision of peace with humanity to include the whole planet.

This transition toward a planetary government is critical if we are to have peace on this planet. Presently, data compiled by Friends of Earth in the United Kingdom from official sources indicate that we suffer from an international anarchy that allows an ecological pollution of 250,000 tons of sulfuric acid to fall as acid rain in the northern hemisphere each day, contaminating our water system and destroying forests. Each minute, 12,000 tons of carbon dioxide enter the atmosphere, amplifying the greenhouse effect brought about by the destruction of the rain forests. Each hour, approximately 1,800 children die of malnutrition, 1,613 acres of productive dryland become desert, 120 million dollars are wasted in global military expenditures, and 10 tons of nuclear waste per day are generated by the 360 nuclear plants in the world. Each one is a potential Chernobyl waiting to contaminate the world with radioactive fallout. Perpetual warfare wastes our planetary resources and prevents us from the prosperity that could be there for every member of the global family and not just for seven percent of the global family.

This international chaos has created an international paranoia. This is not a peaceful way to live. It disrupts the peace and security of a safe family base. Our children grow up under the threat of instant annihilation. **Without the stabilizing security of planetary peace, every unit of our social system is weakened and disrupted.**

When we talk about peace with community, we have to talk about replacing the law of force with the force of law. I believe we are about to make the shift to a worldwide acceptance of civil and human rights as the internationally accepted standard of morality. This general acceptance of civil and human rights as a value will eventually be established in our consciousness just as formalized slavery and racism are no longer acceptable in our moral consciousness. Just as the United States had to end the violence of the "Wild West" by bringing law and order to the western states, so we must bring a level of order to the world to end the terror and potential world destruction of the "international Wild West" we have created. In this way, all families of the world will benefit and be strengthened. Attempting to solve our international problems by threats and wars of mass murder is simply too primitive.

We have four levels of government in the United States today: city, county, state, and national. One more, an international level of government, will complete the structure to provide a practical base from which planetary peace has a chance to grow. The establishment of respected international law gives time for the quality of inner peace to develop. This inner peace is necessary for lasting and fundamental planetary peace. This is like putting a fence around a small tree so that the deer do not eat it. Past U.S. president Harry Truman once said, "When Kansas and Colorado have a quarrel over water in the Arkansas River, they don't call out the national guard and go to war over it. They bring suit in the Supreme Court of the United States and abide by the decision. There isn't a reason in the world why we can not do that internationally. . . . It will be just as easy for nations to get along in a republic of the world as it is for you to get along in the republic of the United States."

Although the advantages of international law and order are obvious, there are those who are resistant to taking the step. There seems to be a variety of fears connected with making such a transition. Those fearful for their autonomy can't see that internationalism does not mean the end of individual nations. Baseball or football leagues do not mean the end of individual teams. In fact, the leagues better enhance the function of each team. The creation of a musical band does not mean the end of guitars. It means a chance for some beautiful music through the harmony of the different instruments.

A change in attitude is needed before we can establish international order. A key attitude behind the success of the constitutional convention of 1787 was the delegates' commitment toward acknowledging and compromising about the diversity of needs, life-styles, and demographics of the different states they represented. This special willingness to compromise made peace possible. As Benjamin Franklin delicately put it, "I confess that there are several parts of this constitution which I do not at present approve. . . . But I am not sure I shall never approve them. For having lived long, I have experienced many instances of being obliged by better information or fuller consideration, to change opinions even on important subjects, which I once thought were right, but found to be otherwise. It is therefore that the older I grow, the more apt I am to doubt my own judgment, and to pay more respect to the judgment of others. . . . I consent, Sir, to this Constitution, because I expect no better and because I am not sure it is not the best. The opinions I have of its errors, I sacrifice to the public good. . . ."

Peace with humanity means a peace in which all nations, all peoples, and all cultures are recognized and respected as an essential part of humanity. It requires compromise in creating a world order that will treat all justly. To achieve peace with humanity, we need to create the conditions for economic, social, political, and spiritual balance in the world. This peace will lovingly end the historical struggle between the haves and have-nots of this world. Peace with humanity will bring a stable abundance and tranquility for all.

Blessed is the Child of Light
Who doth Study the Book of the Law
For he shall be as a candle
In the darkness of night,
And an island of truth
In a sea of falsehood. . . .
The written Law
Is the instrument by which
The unwritten Law is understood. *(EGP 2)*

Truly, by studying the teachings of ageless
    wisdom
Do we come to know God,
For I tell you truly,
The Great Ones saw God face to face;
Even so,
When we read the Holy Scrolls
Do we touch the feet of God. *(EGP 4)*

5

Peace With Culture

Peace with culture involves experiencing the ancient and present wisdom of all cultures. Through culture, we absorb the great teachings that have been given to us by the spiritual masters of all traditions over the past thousands of years. The Essenes were aware of three approaches to spiritual evolution: the intuitive path of the mystic, the path of studying nature, and the path of studying the works of the great masters through their literature and art. They practiced a combination of all three. They studied the great religious works and the works of the great masters. They applied their intuitive and mystical sense, developed by fasting, prayer, and meditation, to intuiting the consciousness of the great masters. This approach allowed them to comprehend the teachings of ancient culture on a deeper level. The Essenes' evolution was also profoundly enhanced by their understanding of the laws of nature. It was customary for everyone to spend a substantial amount of time in the garden. The Essenes were experts in working with trees, plants, and herbs. Mother Nature was one of their greatest teachers.

Universal culture is important to humanity because it represents the highest ideals from all cultures throughout all history. It allows us to connect with the universality of all approaches brought to this planet by the various masters. Those who are unbiased and not threatened by outward differences can see that, at the core, all teachings have the same ageless wisdom. Knowing this ageless wisdom allows us to tap into the evolution of humanity and gives us the perspective that frees us from having to reinvent the wheel. As we rediscover these ancient teachings, we gain support for our own intuitive insights and spiritual unfolding. Today, much confusion exists in the rapidly expanding field of consciousness as well as in the worldwide fundamentalist movements of all religions, because people's understandings and teachings are not rooted in the soil of the last ten thousand years of universal spiritual teachings. We would do well to think several times before embarking on a spiritual path that is out of harmony with the ageless wisdom, universal morality, and teachings of our universal culture.

The main purpose of studying culture is not to add more factual knowledge, but to open us up to sources of universal wisdom. We can make contact with the eternal thinking body of a great master and thus imbibe his or her understanding. The great works of art of a Leonardo da Vinci or a Michelangelo or the music of a Bach, a Mozart, or a Beethoven reflect the truth of our own Self, the Self of all. The great works of culture are a reflection of the God within all of us.

On another level, peace with our own particular background or culture connects us with our roots. Acknowledging and accepting our roots brings us to a deeper experience of being at peace with ourselves. Knowing our cultural roots affirms our connection with historical humanity and helps us to experience ourselves as part of the planetary organism. People of color in the United States have placed much emphasis on knowing their roots for this reason. Native American spiritual teachers have also placed much emphasis on the remembrance of traditional ways of living. We also sometimes see people who have left the Judeo-Christian tradition to explore other spiritual paths return and attempt to integrate their tradition of birth into the spiritual path that has unfolded for them.

Peace with culture is also a reflection of how we interact with each other within our own immediate national culture. If a culture suppresses the rights of others to be at peace, the peace of the body, mind, and family of everyone will eventually be disturbed. Allowing the expression of joy and peace creates peace within the culture. Peace with culture means allowing the full expression of peace in culture to evolve, and being in harmony with this expression. It means allowing our culture to reflect the eternal truth in us.

Blessed is the Child of Light
Who knoweth his Earthly Mother,
For she is the giver of life.
For know that thy mother is in thee,
And thou art in her.
None can live long,
Neither be happy,
But he who honors his Earthly Mother.
 (EGP 2)

6

Peace With the Earthly Mother

Peace with the Earthly Mother is the foundation of our physical and spiritual existence on this planet. Peace with nature requires us to attune ourselves and be sensitive to our inner nature so that we are able to know nature as an extension of our Self. One aspect of this peace is the ability to resensitize ourselves to nature, to feel her energies, to know and cooperate with her laws, and to become one with them as a natural expression of who we are. Peace with nature entails understanding that we are but one strand in the web of life of Mother Nature. **Nature is a reflection and a reminder of our Creator.** Our love of nature enhances our communion with the Divine.

To be at peace with nature is to accept that, on the physical plane, we are governed by the forces of nature. In understanding this, we discover that our health depends on sunlight, clean air, pure water, healthy food, rest in accordance with the cycles of the day and night, exercise of our physical bodies, and harmony of our mind with our inner and outer nature.

Conserving Topsoil

Every nation of this world is subject to the laws of nature. For example, in the book *Topsoil and Civilization* by Vernon Carter and Tom Dale, a clear link is established between the decline of a civilization and soil erosion destroying its fertility base. Topsoil is defined as nutrient-rich soil that holds moisture and in which our crops grow. It is the basic foundation of our sustenance on this earth. The United States Department of Agriculture has acknowledged a drop of seventy percent in the United States cropland productivity as an unparalleled disaster. Two hundred years ago, the U.S. had twenty-one inches of topsoil. Now there are only six inches of topsoil left. According to Dr. Szekely, "Universal history shows that every nation reached its greatest splendor by following the great law of unity between man and nature." Dr. Szekely points out that history shows that when a nation led a simple life of cooperation with nature, that nation flourished, but when the nation deviated from this unity, it inevitably disintegrated or disappeared. We are but human organisms living in the topsoil, along with all the other organisms. When the topsoil is destroyed, so are we.

This law of unity between humanity and nature was held by the Essenes to be the guide to how we should live in the material world. In the Zend Avesta, an ancient synthesis and expansion of early Sumerian wisdom written by Zarathustra, it was taught that the ideal existence entails always keeping in contact with the forces of nature. This law of unity is the foundation for how we may best organize our life on the planet if we are to have a healthy humanity. At this point in our planetary history, if we are simply to survive, we need to begin to follow the law of unity between humanity and nature. **If we keep trying to break the laws of nature, they will eventually break us.**

Unfortunately, since the beginning of the Industrial Revolution, we seem to have forgotten this law of unity with nature. In the last thirty years alone, we have destroyed more of our environment than all of the previous cataclysmic events of previous civilizations on this planet. We have completely broken this law of unity. We act as if we were separate from nature. We exploit nature rather than act as co-creators with nature. We treat nature as an alien force to be fought and conquered. Driven by greed and the search for profit, we can't seem to comprehend the meaning of the unity between humanity and the rest of this planet.

In 1854, Chief Seattle, in his famous address to the president of the United States, forewarned us concerning the result of not respecting the earth as our mother: "His appetite will devour the earth and leave behind only a desert. . . . Whatever befalls the earth befalls the sons of the earth. If men spit upon the ground, they spit upon themselves. . . . Contaminate your bed, and you will one night suffocate in your own waste."

Because of our ignorance, greed, and alienation, we are actively disrupting the ecology of this planet.

Peace With the Earthly Mother   51

According to statistics compiled from official sources by Friends of the Earth in the United Kingdom, each minute fifty-one acres of tropical forests are destroyed, and fifty tons of fertile topsoil are washed or blown off cropland. Every hour 1,613 acres of productive dryland become desert. Each day 25,000 people die because of water shortage and water contamination, and sixty tons of plastic packaging and 372 tons of fishing nets are dumped into the sea by commercial fishermen. One species becomes extinct every five hours. The greenhouse effect is changing our weather. People have become afraid of our friend the sun because the ozone layer has become thinner. Famine has become a regular phenomenon as desert land grows.

Developing the Value
of Peace With Nature

Our present industrial system focuses on the accumulation of wealth rather than on peace with nature. This has caused our nations to forget the unity of humanity and nature. Just one example of the magnitude of this breakdown is the ecological disaster in Poland reported by Sabine Rosenbladt in *Greenpeace* magazine, November–December 1988. In 1985 the Polish parliament recognized four areas of its country as pollution disaster areas, including the Gdansk Bay area, the industrial areas of Upper Silesia, the Krakow area, and the copper basin of Liegnitz/Glogow. By Poland's own industrial standards, these areas are so contaminated with industrial and municipal pollution that the people living in these regions should be evacuated. This represents thirty percent of Poland's population. In the Baltic Sea, seven nations yearly dump 125,000 tons of heavy toxic metals, one million tons of nitrogen, 70,000 tons of phosphorus, and 50,000 tons of oil and highly toxic PCBs. Because of this irresponsibility, Poland's Gdansk Bay, situated on the Baltic Sea, now has 100,000 square kilometers of seafloor that have been declared biologically dead. The fish are almost extinct. One local fisherman said that the last eels that were caught in the bay were so corroded by toxic chemicals that "they looked like they were already cooked." The drinking water of Gdansk is so polluted that one Polish environmentally concerned biophysicist said that the term "drinking water," as a label for what comes out of the tap, is used only for the sake of nostalgia. According to the official 1984 Polish statistics, seventy-one percent of the nation's drinking water was disqualified by the national public health authorities for hygienic reasons. Some people predict that by the year 2000, none of Poland's water will be clean enough to be used for anything. In Krakow, one of the other disaster areas, the life span is three to four years shorter than that of the rest of the population. The rate of cancer in Krakow, especially of lung cancer, is higher than in other areas, as is the rate of allergies, chronic bronchitis, degenerative bone diseases, circulatory illnesses, and infant mortality. In Glogow, another disaster area, contaminated fields continue to be farmed. Twenty percent of the food tested from these areas were classified as hazardous to public health by the authorities. Vegetables were found to have 220 times the acceptable limit for cadmium, 165 for zinc, 134 for

Peace With the Earthly Mother   53

lead, 34 for fluorine, and 2.5 times for uranium. Green lettuce grown near Krakow contained 230 milligrams of lead per kilo. These statistics reflect concretely what is meant when humanity and nature are not in harmony. The case of Poland simply points to the worldwide ecological disaster that is currently underway. To create peace in the world requires that we pay attention to our waste products. As an herbalist friend of mine once said, **"Pay attention to your elimination or it will eliminate you."** Peace with the environment requires that we pay attention and do something—now.

The Gaia Hypothesis

Interestingly enough, our own technology has provided us with a new understanding that may inspire us to reestablish our unity with nature. This new insight is called the Gaia hypothesis. NASA has developed an instrument called the telebioscope, which, when placed upon the various spacecrafts, can determine if life exists on various planets. One experiment was to point this telebioscope at our own planet Earth. The data collected showed that the whole planet is not only alive, but that it possesses all the essential characteristics of a single living organism. From these findings, one of the NASA scientists, James Lovelock, developed what he called the Gaia hypothesis, which proposes that our planet is a single living organism that maintains its own homeostasis. Lovelock noted that a slim margin of biophysical conditions on this planet allow life, as we know it, to exist. These biophysical conditions include a delicate stabilization of the chemical composition of the atmosphere, a ratio of mixtures of barometric pressures, heat from the sun, the axis spin rate, and the mineral composition of the ocean. If these or many other variables that maintain life on this planet are shifted more than a slight degree, it would end life on this planet as we know it. Lovelock determined that these conditions necessary to maintain life on the planet are not inherently stable and that under the normal laws of physics and chemistry these conditions should have only lasted a short time. Somehow, something on this planet has been self-regulating and maintaining the equilibrium of these life-giving conditions for the last four billion years. We see this sort of homeostatic equilibrium in the human body. Perhaps the earth is alive! Perhaps we are each equivalent to one cell in this living organism!

The Gaia hypothesis that planet Earth is a single living organism with intelligence and purpose is both new and quite ancient. Ancient cultures often regarded the energies of the earth, all life, all minds, and the cosmos as one, and yet, at the same time multiple manifestations of universal energy. This "new discovery" of the Gaia hypothesis supports our small but growing rediscovery of the unity of humanity and nature.

One of the most exciting movements today is the tremendous ground swell of interest in national and international ecological concerns. In the last few years, so many ecologically oriented organizations and worldwide television programs have emerged that it is difficult to list them all, but many are included in the resource list at the end of the book. The more we get in touch with the law of unity, the more we will be able to realize that the basic foundation for a healthy humanity is peace with nature.

To preserve the planet is to affirm our own divine spirit. It is the affirmation of life—our very own life and meaning.

If we say the Heavenly Father
Dwelleth within us,
Then are the heavens ashamed;
If we say he dwelleth without us,
It is a falsehood.
The eye which scanneth the far horizon
And the eye which seeth the hearts of men,
He maketh as one eye.
He is not manifest,
He is not hidden.
He is not revealed,
Nor is he unrevealed.
My children, there are no words
To tell that which he is. . . .
He who hath found peace
With his Heavenly Father
Hath entered the Sanctuary
Of the Holy Law. . . .
For in the beginning was the Law,
And the Law was with God,
And the Law was God.
May the Sevenfold Peace
Of the Heavenly Father
Be with thee always. *(EGP 2)*

7

Peace With the Heavenly Father

Peace with God is total peace. It is the totality of the six aspects of peace combined with the transcendental awareness of the One. Peace with God is the indescribable caress of the Divine that we experience in the depth of our soul. It comes from a deep love communion with God. It is the direct knowing of the original thought: I Am. When we become one with ourselves, we become unified with the Universal Divine Law, synergistic with God as a co-creator. We become aligned with cosmic consciousness unfolding on this planet. This awareness manifests as harmony and love on every level of one's life. This state of awareness adds great depth and quality to any world service that we embrace. It is the ultimate starting point for any service. It enhances our ability to see God in every situation. To create peace in the world doesn't require that we be saints right now; it is hard enough without such a requirement. To experience peace with God and all creation just once may be enough to guide and motivate us in this understanding.

The fruition of the other levels of peace are both the cause and effect of this seventh, all-encompassing level of peace. Moving toward this profound level of peace is enhanced by an integration of a variety of efforts, such as eating an appropriate diet for a spiritual life, practicing meditation, exercising, associating with people who are actively developing their spiritual lives, starting all our thoughts with love, actively serving the cause of peace, experiencing the great works of culture, and communing with the forces of nature. These efforts to develop ourselves gradually bring peace with the body and mind. From the base of a peaceful body and mind, and by keeping our hearts open to the vulnerability of intimacy, we develop peace with the family. Peace with humanity naturally develops when there is peace with the body, mind, and family. As our communion with the Divine develops, grace begins to make our efforts flow more easily and bear more fruit. Peace with God gives meaning to the equation of our lives.

Bring unto thy earth the reign of Peace!
Then shall we remember the words
Of him who taught of old the Children of
Light:
I give the peace of the Earthly Mother to
thy body,
And the peace of the Heavenly Father to
thy spirit.
And let the peace of both reign among the
sons of men. . . .
For happy are they that strive for peace,
For they will find the peace of the
Heavenly Father,
And give to everyone thy peace,
Even as I have given my peace unto thee.
For my peace is of God.
Peace be with thee! *(EGP 3)*

8

Integrating Peace on Every Level

The Sevenfold Peace is a Western approach to total peace. It is different from simply residing in a cave and blissing out on cosmic consciousness. It is an active peace in which we operate on every level to enhance the peace in our world and in ourselves. It entails living a spiritual, yet practical, life in the world—not a passive, doormat, not-rocking-the-boat, pseudopeaceful life, but a life in which every action is filled with integrity, regardless of the potential for rejection. The peaceful life is not necessarily easy at this time in history. Mahatma Gandhi felt a life of nonviolent peacefulness required more courage than any other.

A peacemaker turns every moment into an experience of harmony and peace. When we are serving peace, we actively create peace with ourselves, with the family, with humanity, and with the total planetary organism. Serving peace means we feel complete union with all that is. Even if we are graced with a few minutes each day of this synergistic peace experience, it is more than enough.

We need a balance between the nondual merging in the Divine Communion in which we lose our self and let go of body-consciousness, and the practical self-consciousness and body-consciousness that we need in order to operate physically in the world. In our lives today, most of us have unfortunately become self-centered and separate beyond the safety point necessary to preserve the life of our physical instrument. This unnecessary separation from God within ourselves and others creates a feeling of lack because we do not experience the noncausal joy of Divine Communion. This limited reality of separation and duality consciousness deprives us from experiencing the abundance of the universe, the source of all material and spiritual resources, and love itself. This "I" and "thine" approach creates a fundamental disharmony in our relationship to every aspect of life on this planet and in this universe. In this state of disharmony, we mistakenly think we need to conquer and dominate to survive, rather than to live by the abundance created from love. The unity awareness of the Sevenfold Peace helps us to shift away from this excessive self-centeredness to the peaceful dance of love with all of creation. In this state, there is no lack; there is only abundance for all of the earth and its creatures. The Essenes, who lived this way as a culture, always experienced abundance.

The Sevenfold Peace is not simply an intellectual construct. It is an active, daily practice of contemplation and action. It is an active effort to apply the wisdom of the mind and love of the heart to our social, cultural, earthly, and cosmic world. To the Essenes, harmony meant peace. The goal of the Sevenfold Peace is to create harmony in all seven levels of peace in our lives. World peace will come faster if the Sevenfold Peace is put into practice in our own immediate lives and environment. There is no contradiction between manifesting the Sevenfold Peace in our personal lives and working to bring the world into harmony by specific political efforts to improve the world through social action such as the ecology, human rights, and antinuclear movements. The important point, however, is that for peace to be lasting we must go beyond simply working against something done by the "bad guys." The integrated awareness of the Sevenfold Peace supports us in not becoming caught in this dualistic trap. Working on these different levels of peace goes on simultaneously as we evolve. It is not like constructing a building, where one has to build each floor completely before going on to the next. Gently, and with time, our own contradictions and lack of harmony will be examined and brought into harmony.

Resistance to Peace

When physicist J. Robert Oppenheimer was asked by a congressional committee in Washington what we had to do to avoid a nuclear war, he answered clearly, "Make peace." Why do we still ponder the obvious? Why do we hesitate to make peace? Why does creating peace on the planet and in our personal lives seem so complicated? Why, in 1988, was the peace effort in the United States considered one of the ten most under-reported stories by the San Francisco–based Media Alliance? Why do people use the fear of a communist conspiracy to justify acting directly or indirectly against peace? Why do some even invoke the name of God in their resistance to the worldwide peace movement? What infuriates people about others trying to create peace? Why is peace not attractive? Novelist and Holocaust survivor Elie Wiesel, who won the Nobel Peace Prize in 1986, has at least part of the answer to these questions when he says, "Like the patient who dreads leaving his hospital bed, like the prisoner afraid of being taken from his familiar cell, we hesitate, waver: What is at risk is too important. We are afraid to let ourselves go, to allow ourselves to be carried away by wishful thinking."

Lasting peace, to some, seems unreal, a mere flowery concept to which we have aspired for centuries. Even for those of us who talk about peace, do some of us believe on a subtle level that it is *not* possible? The Institute for Noëtic Sciences has pointed out that collectively held unconscious beliefs shape the world's institutions. A collective belief in the possibility of achieving harmonious global peace in our generation contributes to reaching this goal, just as our present collective disbelief thwarts it. It is important that we create the belief in the possibility of peace within ourselves if we are to communicate it to others.

A fundamental cause for the resistance to peace is an inability to see and experience the light of God in others because we either have forgotten the experi-

ence of, or have not yet experienced, that light in ourselves. If we do not know the love of the God Communion within ourselves, how can we love our neighbors as ourselves? Instead, we tend to mistreat our neighbors as we mistreat ourselves.

Another major underlying cause for war is our unconscious search to become whole through the transitory process of subjugating others, rather than through experiencing God Communion. We try to dominate others because we cannot risk seeing others as complete or as fully human because then we might see ourselves as less than human.

War allows us to create the illusion of personal wholeness by dehumanizing or subjugating others. As pointed out in a new and respected classic of social history, *The Chalice and the Blade* by Riane Eisler, war arises either from the need to subjugate others or the need to avoid subjugation. We do not seem to understand our real options for overcoming our sense of incompleteness. The idea of surviving or trying to feel better about ourselves at the expense of others results from this warlike way of thinking.

The work by professor Rene Girard at Stanford adds to this understanding. Due to a "mimetic" or imitative desire, human beings, Girard argues, become addicted to competing with each other to fulfill our artificially instilled desires. The drive to fulfill these desires is another form of trying to feel whole by conquering in the outer world. In this process of competition for our desires, we lose the sense of our oneness. As subsocieties, whole societies, or even nations, we regard each other as obstacles to the gratification of our desires. A meltdown of the social order begins when law and custom cannot contain the hostility. Historically, the way groups or nations have handled this is by the mechanism of scapegoating. The scapegoat can be an individual person—for example, the "identified patient" we sometimes see in family dynamics. Or the scapegoat can include a whole culture, as was the case of the Jews in Germany, or the anti-Semitism and racism that arise in times of economic stress. Scapegoating results in legitimized and actual human sacrifice. Although explicit human sacrifice is taboo, through the process of moral justification, it creeps back into our daily history. Two major forms of the human sacrificial cult that are not recognized as such are war and the execution of criminals. These forms allow social anonymity in the participation in actual human sacrifice and usually serve to bring society back into unity. By proclaiming their moral guilt, as is easy to do with criminals, or the fabricated moral culpability of the "communists" of the cold war, or of anyone who stands in the way of what we want, or of the possible Viet Cong among the villagers of the infamous My Lai massacre, to justify the mass human sacrifice that occurred there, or the drug-dealing evilness of a Noriega or a Qaddafi, or the supposed danger to security of a Sandinista Nicaragua or socialist Grenada, or our historical witch hunts, crusades, racist hangings, or pogroms, we become morally anesthetized to our actual practice of human sacrifice. This only works, however, when people accept the legitimacy of the cult of human sacrifice as the way to solve the problem of desire, rivalry, and internal social disunity. When we understand that the path to wholeness of the individual or the nation is not through the temporary mechanism of scapegoating of an individual, a culture, or nation, then this cultic pseudosolution will no longer work. Our society will no longer be willing to become anesthetized by the surface scapegoat thinking that the media subjects us to, such as the idea that we must "kill to stop the killing" or the fabricated or real moralistic impugning of the targeted scapegoat to "justify" the human sacrifice. The task of the peacemaker is to live in a way that undermines the legitimacy of sacrificial cults and their mob psychology. As peacemakers, we must also live in a personal way that demonstrates that the long-term path to wholeness does not consist of subjugating or sacrificing our neighbors.

Fortunately, we are beginning to recognize that the pattern of unconsciously searching for wholeness through dominating others is dysfunctional on a personal, national, and global level. **We are becoming less willing to participate in actions that do not promote real wholeness and well-being. Our paradigm is shifting toward establishing real paths to wholeness and well-being that do not depend on the illusory and short-lived means of subjugating others. For this reason, we will all eventually achieve a Sevenfold Peace.**

Just as overt legalized discrimination and slavery became obsolete because these practices no longer promoted the feeling of well-being for the majority, so a paradigm shift is emerging toward democracy and civil rights as a basic fundamental human right. In 1989, the world was outraged at the Chinese leadership for slaughtering thousands of students in Tiananmen

Square who were protesting for civil rights and democracy. This is in contrast to a much slower and quieter world reaction to the Chinese Cultural Revolution in the 1960s, in which millions were killed or imprisoned. Eastern Europe's sunburst of light toward establishing independent national democracies and the Soviet Union's new openness to rival parties in a democratic electoral process as we entered the 1990s are examples of this thought-form change. Although these events do not guarantee the establishment of peace, because this is primarily a political and economic shift toward civil rights rather than a sevenfold shift, they do represent a big step.

Peace is inevitable because it is our true inherent nature. It is a mistake to assume that modes of thinking that stem from selfishness and false self-preservation can ever give us a permanent sense of wholeness. Real peace on every level remains eternally open to us as a path for achieving wholeness in our lives. We can approach this through whatever religion or whatever spiritual context we find meaningful. **Paradoxically, the primary motivation for war and for peace is the same—the desire for wholeness.** One of these paths is illusory and temporary, and the other gives us everything. Only through essential peace on every level will the quest for wholeness, primal Divine nurturance, and noncausal joy be fulfilled.

It is not easy to feel whole, to open to the experience of God Communion, to keep our hearts open, to love unconditionally, and to operate in the consciousness of the Sevenfold Peace in our daily lives. For some, it may seem easier to avoid trying to achieve this feeling of wholeness rather than risk failure. Fortunately, in our personal and international relationships, we are beginning to recognize that it is dysfunctional to keep pursuing the illusion of wholeness through subjugating or overpowering others. At this point in history, our challenge is to search for true wholeness. Some, however, are afraid of the experience of the light of the Divine within. For some of us, just the experience of being quiet may be threatening, because in those quiet moments we fear we will get in touch with some parts of ourselves we do not want to experience. Others of us fear the inner world because it is uncharted and undefined. Still others are afraid of the immensity and expansive universal feeling of wholeness. Because we have never known this primary nurturing experience of the Divine, some of us do not believe it is possible.

Many others have lost touch with the mystical experience of oneness and wholeness. When faced with the possibility of inner silence, it seems easier to start a holy crusade than to face the fear of the inner experience. It is as if a conditioned fear reflex gets activated that covers up our essential experience of wholeness with God. I see this all the time in participants in my Tree of Life seminars. These seminars are designed to stimulate the awakening to Divine Communion and the Sevenfold Peace. I can often feel the resistance in people; sometimes it's an absolute terror of letting go, often just some hesitation about letting go and surrendering to a greater awareness than our limiting ego. In my own preliminary awakening in 1972, I felt an agonizing hour of the fear of the mystical unknown. This experience has made it easier for me to recognize it in others. Once this fear is acknowledged, it is amazing how easily and quickly most people, with just a little support, pass through it in a few minutes or hours. If we do not acknowledge the fear and face it, it sometimes takes a longer time to break through.

One of the most basic resistances to peace is human inertia. Many people do not value peace enough to want to make the effort necessary to bring about inner changes. Who likes to give up their comforts? It is, indeed, uncomfortable in some ways to change one's life-style. This is especially true when we do not feel any direct pain from it, such as a cigarette smoker or coffee drinker often does. Peace is not perceived as a dramatic or urgent issue, like a famine in Africa, and so it is easy not to make it an active priority in our lives. The inertia manifests even in something relatively minor like adapting the peaceful practice of a vegetarian diet, which directly helps to save the rain forests and preserve the ecology, or living in other ways that will support planetary survival. The great Indian spiritual master Meher Baba speaks to this dilemma eloquently in *Message by Meher Baba: The Religion of Life*: "He has got entangled in the superficiality of rigid forms and ceremonies, seeking consolation in mechanical ritualism and evading the drastic results of applied Truth. As Truth is the very negation of the ego-life, to which man desperately clings, he tries to escape from the deeper perceptions of his own Higher Self, ardently praying for Light in some form of Church, but resisting it in everyday practical life, in numberless ways. Afraid of the flooding forces of Light, which his own prayers have released, man seeks to perpetuate his ego-life, by embracing self-delusion and by clinging to word rather than meaning, to form rather than spirit. He cannot wholeheartedly accept Truth; nor can he wholeheartedly accept ignorance. So he takes shelter in high sounding words and comforting slogans, misleading himself and others, thinking that he is following Light, when in reality, he is resisting it. But the pseudo-light which he seems to get through fanatic allegiance to non-understood dogma, cannot give him real peace; nor can it eternally fortify him against the purifying and redeeming forces of the living Truth, which he has invited upon himself, through moments of sincere prayer and earnest search. Not being able to reconcile himself with Light or with Darkness, man seeks to entrench his ego-life by taking his stand in the illusory and penumbral realm of merely verbal learning, which is like a mirage that only arrests further search for real water, without in any way allaying his thirst."

Creating peace requires an effort by all of us to overcome our inertia even on what seems the smallest level. In southern California, people complained when the antipollution program went beyond stricter control of industries and auto pollution into their own backyards. They did not like it when their polluting gasoline-powered lawn mowers and barbecues were included. In the San Francisco Bay Area, the *San Francisco Chronicle* reported it took a U.S. District Judge to order a crackdown on pollution caused by household products such as cleaners, aerosols, deodorants, insect sprays, furniture polishes, and air fresheners. Because the reductions in the use of household pollutants in the San

Francisco Bay Area were to be made by 1985, the judge castigated state officials for their "appalling failure" to act sooner and gave them until 1993 to reduce consumer polluting solvents by four tons a day. **Honestly acknowledging our resistance to the changes needed for a more peaceful life-style allows us to boldly face our inertia and inspire ourselves to overcome it.**

Developing the heartful willingness to share the resources of the world in some more equal way between the haves and have-nots is even more threatening. Our greedy and automaton desires to hang onto our addictions and to the familiar ways that bring direct and indirect violence to ourselves and the rest of the planet create a tremendous resistance to peace. **Living peacefully on every level is not necessarily easy, but it is profoundly worth it.** There are great subtle rewards when we change our life-style habits away from those that directly or indirectly support a warlike attitude or actions toward humanity and the planet. There is an opening up and a freeing of energy; a joy emerges that makes us come alive and makes our lives intensely meaningful.

Simple Ways to Overcome Inertia and Make Peace

Institutions alone cannot save the earth from the cumulative results of our everyday, seemingly unimportant inner thoughts and life-style actions or lack of actions. Sometimes, we feel helpless in the face of the apparent power of governments or large corporations. But remember, governments and corporations are made up of people, and they depend on people for their power. We are those people. Our seemingly unimportant thoughts and actions *do* make a difference. Our collective daily choices about how we live on this planet have a profound impact. Someday, if we all participate in changing our own lives, we will make a significant difference, and peace will prevail on earth.

PEACE WITH THE BODY

1. Choose to take responsibility for your own personal health and improve the ecology of your personal body just as you would care for the planet. (a) Exercise aerobically at least three times per week for one-half hour; brisk walking is sufficient. (b) Practice deep breathing three times a day with ten cycles of four counts inhalation, sixteen counts hold, and eight counts exhalation. This 1:4:2 ratio can be increased in length. Ninety percent of our energy comes from oxygen. (c) Get sufficient sleep and relaxation. (d) Drink pure water.

2. Peace with the planetary body. (a) If you are not a vegetarian already, read *Diet for a New America* by John Robbins and consider the ramifications of eating flesh food on the planetary ecology and peace in general. The flesh-food industry accounts for over fifty percent of our water usage, eighty-five percent of soil loss, and twenty times more land usage than that required for a vegan diet. A vegan diet saves one acre of trees per year. (b) At your own rate, add vegetarian food and progressively cut out red meat, poultry, and fish from your diet. (c) Support local farmers' markets; their produce usually has less pesticide residue and

is fresher. (d) Buy certified organically grown produce on a regular basis. This preserves bodily health, soil fertility, and wildlife, and minimizes soil loss and water pollution.

3. Peace with the cosmic body. Think about yourself as one cell in the cosmic body. Instead of thinking about humanity as the web of life, begin to understand humanity as one strand in the cosmic web of life.

PEACE WITH THE MIND

1. Enhance your own inner peace by learning to meditate or pray. Keep asking, do I "barter that which is eternal for that which dieth in an hour"?

2. Enhance peace with the planetary mind by thinking positive thoughts and participating in some thought form for peace group activity such as World Healing Hour on December 31st, Peace the 21st on each equinox or solstice, or on the last day of the month, or take time daily at noon or 7 A.M. in meditations for peace. According to *The Maharishi Effect*, data from a summer project in Rhode Island showed that one group of 350 people meditating daily on peace decreased the amount of social disorder by forty percent.

3. Enhance peace with the cosmic mind by trying to begin each thought, word, and action with love.

PEACE WITH THE FAMILY

1. Forgive everybody. Forgiveness ends the memory and depletes the energy of conflict.

2. Love your neighbor as your Divine self. If you're not sure whether you or your neighbor have a Divine

self, pretend that both of you do and try relating from that understanding.

PEACE WITH HUMANITY

1. Make a point to volunteer or contribute to humanitarian causes and organizations. Check with any local peace center for a list of causes and ways to contribute. Volunteers are much appreciated by almost all of these groups. See the resource list at the end of the book for ideas.

2. Develop your livelihood so that it supports your personal and planetary values. Start this one step at a time. This may take several years, so be patient and persistent.

3. Begin socially responsible investing (SRI), which is investing in organizations with positive community and environmental policies. Get a credit card, mutual fund, and/or a checking account with a SRI policy. For information on SRI companies, ask your investment counselor, bank, or credit union.

4. Become a peacemaker in all levels of your life and inspire others to do the same. Let your life be an example of living your ideals. The cumulative effect of your inspiring your friends, and your friends inspiring a wider circle, will transform our social, economic, governmental, and religious institutions and bring peace to the world

PEACE WITH CULTURE

1. Participate in art, music, drama, or other cultural events that inspire and connect you with the eternal

values of love, peace, beauty, truth, and the Divine in all.

2. Make peace with your own cultural roots. Ask your parents or grandparents for stories about your cultural origins. Read a book about them or take a class on your culture of origin.

3. Try to respect and appreciate the flourishing of peace and joy in all cultures.

4. Explore activities that bring you into harmony with the culture of nature's rhythms. It is not surprising that most cultures have such rituals.

PEACE WITH THE EARTHLY MOTHER/ECOLOGY

1. Commit yourself to planting one or more trees this year. If you do not know how to plant and care for a tree, call a local nursery for instructions. According to *50 Simple Things You Can Do to Save the Earth*, the average American uses up the equivalent of seven trees per year. It also points out that if every American family planted one tree per year, over a billion pounds of "greenhouse gases" would be removed from the air per year. Planting seven trees each year keeps us ecologically even. Because trees absorb large quantities of carbon dioxide, they help to prevent the greenhouse effect, provide oxygen, help to preserve the soil, and are uplifting to the spirit.

2. Recycle all newspapers, glass, aluminum, tin, organic refuse, and anything else you are able to recycle creatively. Recycling has a powerful conservation effect on our environment. According to *50 Simple Things You Can Do to Save the Earth*, if everyone in the

United States recycled even one-tenth of their newspapers, we would save about twenty-five million trees per year. **Small steps multiplied by millions do make a difference.**

3. Support environmental groups by volunteering or with donations.

4. Participate in the "campaign for the earth," which is a unifying symbolic idea, not an organization, for individuals and groups around the world who are committed to working to heal the planet, and ourselves as part of that process. The campaign involves acting as part of the vision of healing the earth. Identify with the vision with your own unique action and thoughts. Share the vision with others. Acknowledge yourself as a citizen of the earth.

5. Read and act on *50 Simple Things You Can Do to Save the Earth.*

PEACE WITH THE HEAVENLY FATHER/GOD

1. Find your own personal way to connect with the Divine every day.

The Full Peace of Wholeness Is Fun

Although the essence of most spiritual teachings gives a different message, most people have been programmed to believe that the way to attain happiness, and therefore peace, is through some sort of external achievement. Some form of domination is involved in striving for peace, whether it's by accumulating lots of money and external trophys of material success, winning in athletic competition, rising to the top of the corporation or union, winning political elections, winning a war, subduing the environment, shopping, or controlling other people in relationships or through organizational structures. These approaches may work for a little while. I remember as captain of an undefeated college football team how whole and good I would feel after dominating another team. I also recall how hard I would work to win again the next week so I could again feel good, or at least not feel bad. Spectators are one step removed from the same process of trying to feel whole through the winning of their team. Sometimes, for example, in the Superbowl or hometown college football games, the spectators get as "high" about the game as the players. One day I simply woke up and saw this endless conscious/unconscious search for an external event to make me feel whole for the illusion that it was, and I stopped. This does not mean that I melted forever into an inactive, blissful lump on the floor. I continue to be as active as before, but now I am primarily motivated by my intuitive attunement with my role on the planet at this time.

We are now called a nation of addicts by many experts. Our affluent culture has found many external ways to, at least temporarily, relieve the feeling of discontent and lack of wholeness. Overeating and drug taking are just two of the more predominant ways. But it is not just drugs, food, relationships, or other forms of domination to which we are addicted; we are addicted to the search for the experience of peace and wholeness. Our addictions arise because we are involved in an endless repetitious array of external activities in an effort to attain a permanent experience of peace and happiness. The problem is that peace, happiness, and wholeness cannot be found on a permanent basis through external activities. They require a shift from external manipulation to the internal quest. I once heard a true story by someone who realized this point through a series of experiences. After he finished the excitement of athletics in college, he began to feel empty and bored. To alleviate this, he took up motorcycle riding, which gave him some temporary happiness. When that didn't work anymore, he took up downhill skiing, which made him feel okay for a few years. When skiing stopped working for him, he went in for skydiving. This worked for a while until he broke both legs in a poor landing. At this point, he decided there must be a more direct way to feel happy and whole. His search led him to experience the Divine in meditation. Saint Augustine, in his autobiography *The Confessions*, describes this moment of change: "Thou hast made us for thyself, O Lord, and our hearts are restless until they rest in thee."

The source from which all peace grows is our experience of the Divine in our lives. Many people first experience the Divine within; then, as a seed grows, it permeates our outer experience. Others first begin to develop a process of sacramental awareness (sense of the holy) in which the boundary between outer and inner lessens through meditation on scriptures, nature, persons, or events. This experience of wholeness brings a spontaneously arising contentment, inner calm, tranquility, and harmony with, and as, the One. This awareness cannot be fully communicated, but it can be pointed toward. Each person experiences it in his or her own way and language.

The experience of Divine Communion entails a feeling of total, abundant fullness with God. A person with such an awareness lives a life that is full of the sweet presence of the Divine with every breath. He or she is made sublimely content with the daily kiss of all the angels of the Earthly Mother and Heavenly Father. Love pulses in every bodily cell, nurtured by the essential peace of all creation. The energies of all the forces of life tingle through the body with a quiet excitement; they flow through the body in the exquisite harmony of the One as we live our daily activities. A joy without cause bubbles from the heart. **With every breath, with every sound, with every moment, the one at peace is bathed in the inner nectar of love. A life of peace is fun.** As the great Sufi poet Rumi put it, "The man of God is drunken [God-intoxicated] while sober. The man of God is full without meat [food]."

The more we experience this subtle "intoxication," the more it becomes a sustained awareness in us. We meditate to reclaim the primary awareness that we are love and wholeness, and from this the rest of the peace work will follow naturally.

Isaiah 30:15 states, "In sitting still and rest shall you be saved, in quietness and confidence will be your strength." Prayer, good fellowship, and service with the awareness of the Divine in our brothers and sisters are also powerful ways to reclaim the primary experience of the One. The full practice of the consciousness of the Sevenfold Peace is an important aid to this sustained experience of wholeness, because it was developed for bringing us into harmony. It is probably why the Essenes were able to sustain their communities in such profound peace for so many hundreds of years.

The Practice of the Sevenfold Peace

The Essenes contemplated one of the principles of the Sevenfold Peace at noontime each day. On Saturday, they focused on transcendental awareness; on Sunday, peace with the kingdom of nature; on Monday, peace with culture; on Tuesday, peace with humanity or social peace; on Wednesday, peace with the family; on Thursday, peace with the mind; and on Friday, peace with the body. On Saturday, in addition to focusing on the Divine, one of the other six aspects is also contemplated all day long. The whole Sevenfold Peace cycle takes seven weeks. This gentle practice helps us to maintain a conscious awareness of the living of peace in our lives. To create peace for ourselves and this world requires some effort. Yet, paradoxically, total peace is not an automatic result of circumstances or practices. Total peace happens beyond the bonds of linear, causal process, through the intangibility of grace. Grace and effort are like two sides of a coin.

Conclusion

It is estimated that within the next few decades the deterioration of the earth's life support systems will accelerate at such a rate that none of our present mild efforts at conservation will be able to save us. The tropical forests that are our earth's lungs are too rapidly being destroyed, and the oceans, rivers, and the other waterways that are our earth's circulation system are becoming so polluted that the earth as an organism is becoming toxic. The flesh of our earthly topsoil is being scraped so thin that it will no longer be able to support us. As of 1990, regardless of a steadily increasing global warming from the greenhouse effect, the United States and Japan at a seventy-one nation conference on global warming were unwilling even to sign an agreement to limit carbon dioxide emissions to their present excessive daily level. Carbon dioxide emissions are considered a major cause of the greenhouse effect. We are like a global alcoholic who is unable to stop drinking as his body and mind deteriorate from the toxicity of the alcohol. Will the people on this planet choose to be so attached to their destructive habits and consumptive life-style that they would rather die than give them up? Or, in an act of sanity and spiritual awareness, will there be a mass human awakening to our condition and to the need for peace on every level? Will we choose to sober up? Will we choose to wake up and heal ourselves on a global level? **Nothing less than the full Sevenfold Peace is worth working for at this time, because nothing less will be strong enough medicine to heal this planet. What is necessary is a commitment to total peace on every level.**

The way toward peace is to make peace the way in every cell of our body and on all seven levels of our lives. At the same time, it requires us to commit to one genuine step at a time, to commit to actions we feel in our hearts that we can honestly make and sustain. To set goals for changes in ourselves that are beyond our capacity can lead to confusion and discouragement for ourselves and for those to whom we have made the commitments. For us to become peacemakers, we need the self-will to overcome our own inertia, fear, and apathy toward creating peace. Our job then becomes to inspire people out of their apathy toward peace, to dispel ignorance, to overcome our subtle disbelief and fear of the experience of peace, to start every thought and action with love, and to bring this love and peace to every situation the best we can. **To create peace in our own lives, our beliefs and the way we live must come into alignment. In this way we create peace by being peace.**

Collectively we can and will, with God's grace, heal ourselves and the soul of this planet.

And all shall work together
In the garden of the Brotherhood
Yet each shall follow his own path
And each shall commune with his own heart.

Though the brothers be of different complexion
Yet do they all toil
In the vineyard of the Earthly Mother
And they all do lift their voice together
In praise of the Heavenly Father

There shall be no peace among peoples
Till there be one garden of the brotherhood
Over the earth. (EGP 2)

References

This list includes titles mentioned in this book as well as sources for the various statistics cited.

Ambassadors of Peace: A Dialogue at the United Nations Between Dr. Robert Muller and Sant Darshan Singh. Costa Rica University for Peace, 1988.

Aron, Elaine, and Aron, Arthur. *The Maharishi Effect: A Revolution Through Meditation.* Walpole, NH: Stillpoint Publishing, 1986.

Baba, Meher. *Message by Meher Baba: The Religion Of Life.* Seattle, WA: W.C. Healy Press, 1945.

Cousens, Gabriel. *Spiritual Nutrition and the Rainbow Diet.* Boulder, CO: Cassandra Press, 1986.

Culi, Yaakov Rabbi. *The Torah Anthology.* New York: Maznaim Publishing Corporation, 1977.

de Mallac, Guy. *Gandhi's Seven Steps to Global Change.* Santa Fe, NM: Ocean Tree Books, 1987.

Ferencz, Benjamin B., and Keyes, Ken, Jr. *Planethood: The Key to Your Survival and Prosperity.* Coos Bay, OR: Vision Books.

Friends of Peace Pilgrim. *Peace Pilgrim.* Santa Fe, NM: Ocean Tree Books, 1982.

Greenpeace [magazine], vol. 6, no. 6 (November–December 1988) and vol. 14, no. 1 (January–February 1989).

Helminski, Edmund. (Trans.) *The Ruins of the Heart: Selected Lyric Poetry of Jelaluddin Rumi.* Putney, VT: Threshold Books, 1981.

Journal of the American Medical Association. "Diet and Stress in Vascular Disease." *JAMA*, vol. 176, no. 9 (June 3, 1961).

Mayer, Jean. *Dietary Goals for the U.S.* Cited by the U.S. Senate Select Committee on Nutrition and Human Needs. Washington DC, February 1977.

Nisbet, Robert. *History of the Idea of Progress.* New York: Basic Books, 1980.

Pearse, Innes H., and Crocker, Lucy H. *The Peckham Experiment: A Study of the Living Structure of Society.* Rushden, Great Britain: Northamptonshire Printing and Publishing Co., 1947.

Phillips, R. "Coronary Heart Disease Mortality Among Seventh Day Adventists With Differing Dietary Habits." *The American Journal of Clinical Nutrition.* Abstract, American Public Health Association Meeting, Chicago, November 16–20, 1975.

Robbins, John. *Diet for a New America.* Walpole, NH: Stillpoint Publishing, 1987.

Russell, Peter. *The Global Brain: Speculations on the Evolutionary Leap to Planetary Consciousness.* Los Angeles: J. P. Tarcher, 1983.

Schwartz, Richard H. *Judaism and Vegetarianism.* Marblehead, MA: Micah Publications, 1988.

St. Augustine. *The Confessions.* Washington, DC: Catholic University Press, 1953.

Szekely, Edmond Bordeaux. *The Essenes by Josephus and His Contemporaries.* U.S.: International Biogenic Society, 1981.

———. *The Essene Gospel of Peace, Book 1.* U.S.: International Biogenic Society, 1981.

———. *The Essene Gospel of Peace, Book 2: The Unknown Books of the Essenes.* U.S.: International Biogenic Society, 1981.

———. *The Essene Gospel of Peace, Book 3: Lost Scrolls of the Essene Brotherhood.* U.S.: International Biogenic Society, 1981.

———. *The Essene Gospel of Peace, Book 4: The Teachings of the Elect.* U.S.: International Biogenic Society, 1981.

———. *From Enoch to the Dead Sea Scrolls.* U.S.: International Biogenic Society, 1981.

———. *The Essene Way: Biogenic Living.* U.S.: International Biogenic Society, 1981.

The Earth Works Group. *50 Simple Things You Can Do to Save the Earth.* Berkeley, CA: Earthworks Press, 1989.

Vaughan, Frances, and Walsh, Roger. (Eds.) *A Gift of Peace: Selections From a Course in Miracles.* New York: St. Martin's Press, 1986.

Vegetarian Times, Issue 152 (April 1990). Published by Vegetarian Life and Times, Inc. (Illinois).

References   87

Suggested Readings

I highly recommend all of the books listed here. The Essene Gospel of Peace volumes can be ordered through the International Biogenic Society (IBS), Box 205, Matsqui, British Columbia, Canada VOX 1SO.

Cousens, Gabriel. *Spiritual Nutrition and the Rainbow Diet*. Boulder, CO: Cassandra Press, 1986.

de Mallac, Guy. *Gandhi's Seven Steps to Global Change*. Santa Fe, NM: Ocean Tree Books, 1987.

Ferencz, Benjamin B., and Keyes, Ken, Jr. *Planethood: The Key to Your Survival and Prosperity*. Coos Bay, OR: Vision Books.

Friends of Peace Pilgrim. *Peace Pilgrim*. Santa Fe, NM: Ocean Tree Books, 1982.

Hubbard, Barbara Marx. *The Evolutionary Journey: A Personal Guide to a Positive Future*. San Francisco: Evolutionary Press, 1982. Distributed by Island Pacific Northwest.

Robbins, John. *Diet for a New America*. Walpole, NH: Stillpoint Publishing, 1987.

Szekely, Edmond Bordeaux. *The Essene Gospel of Peace, Book 1*. U.S.: International Biogenic Society, 1981.

_____ . *The Essene Gospel of Peace, Book 2: The Unknown Books of the Essenes*. U.S.: International Biogenic Society, 1981.

_____ . *The Essene Gospel of Peace, Book 3: Lost Scrolls of the Essene Brotherhood*. U.S.: International Biogenic Society, 1981.

_____ . *The Essene Gospel of Peace, Book 4: The Teachings of the Elect*. U.S.: International Biogenic Society, 1981.

_____ . *From Enoch to the Dead Sea Scrolls*. U.S. International Biogenic Society, 1981.

_____ . *The Essene Way: Biogenic Living*. U.S.: International Biogenic Society, 1981.

The Earth Works Group. *50 Simple Things You Can Do to Save the Earth*. Berkeley, CA: Earthworks Press, 1989.

Vaughan, Frances, and Walsh, Roger. (Eds.) *A Gift of Peace: Selections From a Course in Miracles*. New York: St. Martin's Press, 1986.

Resource List

Ecology

Center for Marine Conservation
1725 DeSales St. NW
Washington, DC 20036

Citizens' Clearinghouse for
Hazardous Waste
P.O. Box 926
Arlington, VA 22216

Citizens for a Better Environment
33 East Congress, Suite 523
Chicago, IL 60605

Citizens for a Better Environment
942 Market St., Suite 505
San Francisco, CA 94102

Conservation International
1015 18th St. NW
Washington, DC 20036

Die Verbraucher Initiative
Koinstr 198
Postfach 17 46
5300 Bonn 1, West Germany
(02 28) 65 90 44

Earth Garden Project
Transculture, Inc.
496 Hudson St. #826
New York, NY 10014

Earth Island Institute
300 Broadway, Suite 28
San Francisco, CA 94133

EarthSave
315 Quail Terrace
Ben Lomond, CA 95005
(408) 423-4069

Environmental Defense Fund
1616 P St. NW, Suite 150
Washington, DC 20036

Environmental Policy Institute
218 D St.
Washington, DC 20003
(202) 544-2600

Friends of the Earth
530 7th St. SE
Washington, DC 20003
(202) 543-4312

Greenhouse Crisis Foundation
1130 17th St. NW, Suite 630
Washington, DC 20036

Greenpeace, USA
Headquarters
1436 U St. NW
Washington, DC 20009
(202) 462-1177

Green Program Project
P.O. Box 111
Burlington, VT 05402

International Union for
Conservation of Nature and
Natural Resources
Gland 1196, Switzerland

International Wildlife Coalition
1807 H St. NW, Suite 301
Washington, DC 20006
(202) 347-0822

Japan Public Citizen
9th Floor, Central Building
1-1-5 Kyobashi, Chuo-Ku
Tokyo, 104, Japan
(03) 272-3900

National Audubon Society
645 Pennsylvania Ave. SE
Washington, DC 20003

National Wildlife Federation
1412 16th St. NW
Washington, DC 20036

Natural Resources Defense Council
40 West 20th St.
New York, NY 10011

Nature Conservancy International
1800 North Kent St., Suite 800
Arlington, VA 22209

New Forests Fund
731 Eighth St.
Washington, DC 20003

New Zealand Nuclear Free Zone
  Committee
Box 18541
Christchurch 9 New Zealand
889-816

Nuclear Awareness Project
730 Bathhurst St.
Toronto, Ontario, Canada M5S 2R4
(416) 537-0438

Oceanic Society
218 D St. SE
Washington, DC 20003

Rainforest Action Network
300 Broadway, Suite 28
San Francisco, CA 94133

Renew America
1001 Connecticut Ave. NW,
  Suite 1719
Washington, DC 20036

Rocky Mountain Institute
1739 Snowmass Creek Rd.
Snowmass, CO 81654

Sane Freeze
711 G Street
Washington, DC 20002

Sierra Club
P.O. Box 7603
San Francisco, CA 94120-9826
(415) 776-2211

SunEnergy
P.O. Box 8371 Symonds
Auckland, New Zealand

Wilderness Society
1400 I St. NW, 10th floor
Washington, DC 20005

World Resources Institute
1735 New York Ave. NW
Washington, DC 20006

Worldwatch Institute
1776 Massachusetts Ave. NW
Washington, DC 20036

World Wildlife Fund
1250 24th St. NW, 5th floor
Washington, DC 20037

90   Resource List

Health

American Vegan Society
501 Old Harding Highway
Malaga, NJ 08328

Center for Science in the Public Interest/Americans for Safe Food
1501 16th St. NW
Washington, DC 20036
(202) 332-9110

Citizens Concerned About Food Irradiation
Box 236, Red Hill
Queensland, Australia 4059

First Christians Essene Church
2536 Collier Ave.
San Diego, CA 92116

Food and Water, Inc.
225 Lafayette #612
New York, NY 10012
(212) 941-9340

Food First
1885 Mission St.
San Francisco, CA 94103
(415) 864-8555

Foundation Soleil
Bois des Arts 38
CH 1225 Geneva, Switzerland
022 489676

Internationale Bioenergetic Society (IBS)
Box 205
Matsqui, British Columbia, Canada VOX 1S0

International Organization of Consumer Unions (IOCU)
Box 1045
10830 Penang, Malaysia
(604) 371-396

London Food Commission
Box 291
London, N5 1DU, United Kingdom
(01) 633-578

National Coalition to Stop Food Irradiation
P.O. Box 59-0488
San Francisco, CA 94159
(415) 626-2734

North American Vegetarian Society
P.O. Box 72
Dolgeville, NY 13329

Spiritual Emergence Network
Institute of Transpersonal Psychology
250 Oak Grove Ave
Menlo Park, CA 94025
(415) 327-2776

World Research Foundation
15300 Ventura Blvd., Suite 405
Sherman Oaks, CA 91403
(818) 907-5483

Thought Form for Peace

Group Avatar
P.O. Box 4155
Tucson, AZ 85738

Karuna Foundation
P.O. Box 11422
Berkeley, CA 94701

Operation Planet Love
Calle Adolfo Prieto No. 125-D-501
Col. Del Valle C.P. 03100
Mexico, D.F., Mexico

Peace the 21st
1474 Bathhurst St.
Toronto, Ontario, Canada
  M5P 3G9
(416) 541-5477
FAX: (416) 651-8831

Peace the 21st–Sonoma County
411 Sunnyslope Ave.
Petaluma, CA 94952

Pentagon Meditation Group
4617 Hunt Ave.
Chevy Chase, MD 20815
(301) 656-6614

People for Planetary Peace
845 Via de la Paz
Pacific Palisades, CA 90272
(One hour a month for peace on the last day of each month)

Positive Thinking Planetary
  Network
Anse St. Jean
Quebec, Canada G0V 1J0
(Love Chain, fifteen minutes each Sunday at 12:00 P.M. local time)

Quartus Foundation
P.O. Box 1768
Boerne, TX 78006-6768
(512) 328-0673

Shekum Foundation
5968 Chabot Crest
Oakland, CA 94618
(415) 547-4230

The Noon Fellowship
Box 110
Weston, Ontario, Canada M9N 3M6

The Society of Prayer for World
  Peace
800 3rd Ave., 31st floor
New York, NY 10022
(212) 755-4755

Planetary Peace

Action Linkage
5828 Telegraph
Oakland, CA 94609

African Link
P.O. Box 72723
Ndola, Zambia

American Friends Service
  Committee
1501 Cherry St.
Philadelphia, PA 19102
(215) 241-7000

American Society for the Prevention
  of Cruelty to Animals
441 East 92nd St.
New York, NY 10128
(212) 876-7700

A New American Place
283 Marina Blvd.
San Francisco, CA 94123

Animal Rights International
Box 214
Planetarium Station
New York, NY 10024

Better World Society
1140 Connecticut
Washington, DC 20036

Beyond War
222 High St.
Palo Alto, CA 94301
(415) 851-2626

Center for Soviet American
Dialogue
14426 N.E. 16th Pl.
Bellevue, WA 98003

Center for Sustainable
Development
P.O. Box 120
Ipswich, MA 01938
(508) 768-6742

Centre Link Trust
31 Grove End Rd.
London, NW8 9LY, United
Kingdom

Centro de Amigos Para la Paz
50 M. Este OLJ
San José, Costa Rica
(506) 51-38-49

Children as Peacemakers
950 Battery St.
San Francisco, CA 94111
(415) 981-0916

Christic Institute
1324 North Capitol St. NW
Washington, DC 20002
(202) 797-8106

Clean Water Action Project
317 Pennsylvania Ave.
Washington, DC 20003

Common Cause
2030 M St. NW
Washington, DC 20036

Doves of Peace
3 Lendon Place
Macgregor, Australia

Earth First!
P.O. Box 5871
Tucson, AZ 85703

EarthLight
1226 Jenifer
Madison, WI 53703

EarthLink
P.O. Thora
N.S.W. 2454 Australia

EarthNet
225 Kahoea Pl.
Kula, Maui, HI 96790
(808) 878-2024

Earth Stewards
6330 Eagle Harbor Dr.
Bainbridge Island, WA 98136

Findhorn One-Earth Network
The Park
Forres, IV36 OTZ, Scotland

Fraternidad Universal
P.O. Box 943
Geheregia, Costa Rica
37-2019

Friends of Animals, Inc.
11 West 60th St.
New York, NY 10023
(212) 247-8077

Global Citizen
11886 Claude Court
Northglenn, CO 80233
(303) 457-2465

Global Family
112 Jordan Ave.
San Anselmo, CA 94960
(415) 453-7600

Grassroots International
P.O. Box 312
Cambridge, MA 02139
(617) 497-9180

Green Net
26028 Underwood STR
London, N1 7JQ, United Kingdom

Institute for Planetary Synthesis
P.O. Box 128
CH-1211 Geneva 20 Switzerland

Institute of Noëtic Science
475 Gate Five Road
Sausalito, CA 94965
(415) 331-5650

International Network for U.N.
  Second Assembly
308 Cricklewood Lane
London, NW2 2PX, United
  Kingdom

International Society for Animal
  Rights, Inc.
421 South State St.
Clarks Summit, PA 18411
(717) 586-2200

National Anti-Vivisection Society
100 East Ohio St.
Chicago, IL 60611
(312) 787-4486

Ojai Foundation
P.O. Box 1620
Ojai, CA 93023

One Society
2616 Iron St.
Bellingham, WA 98225
(206) 676-4408

Our Planet in Every Classroom
21 Inglewood Drive
Toronto, Ontario, Canada M4T 1G7
(416) 485-6221

Pax International
43 Rue de Villez, Bennelourt
78270 Bennieres-Sur-Seine, France

Peace Child
3977 Chain Bridge
Fairfax, VA 22030

Peace Is Possible
2008 Grand Ave. S
Minneapolis, MN 55405

Peace Links
747 8th St. SE
Washington, DC 20003

Peacemakers, Inc.
P.O. Box 141254
Dallas, TX 75214
(214) 871-8448

Peace Through Understanding
P.O. Box 95910
2509 CX, The Hague, The
  Netherlands

People for the Ethical Treatment
  of Animals (PETA)
P.O. Box 42516
Washington, DC 20015
(202) 726-0156

Physicians for Social Responsibility
1601 Connecticut Ave.
Washington, DC 20009

Planetary Citizens
325 Ninth St.
San Francisco, CA 94103

Planetary Light Association
P.O. Box 5568
Lynnwood, WA 98046

Planetwork
Box 804
Ketchum, ID 83340
(208) 726-4016

Project Love
688 Rt. 202 South
Flemington, NJ 08822

Public Citizen (Ralph Nader)
2000 P St. NW #605
Washington, DC 20036

Radio Peace
P.O. Box 1143
Arleta, CA 91331

Rotary Peace
1560 Sherman Ave.
Evanston, IL 60201

SEVA Foundation
8 N. San Pedro Rd.
San Rafael, CA 94903
(415) 492-1829

Terre Nouvelle
BP52
05300 Laragne, France
92-652425

The Bristol Group
13, The Drive
Henlease, Bristol, BS9, United
   Kingdom

The Center for Peace
Rt 11, Box 369
Sevierville, TN 37863

The Fund for Animals
200 W. 57th St.
New York, NY 10019
(212) 246-2096

The Peace Curriculum, Inc.
1014 20th Ave., SE
Minneapolis, MN 55414
(612) 623-8012

The Peace Pole Project
P.O. Box 170279
San Francisco, CA 94117
(415) 731-7917
FAX: (415) 731-7923

The University for Peace
Apartado 95 Barrio
San José, 1005 Costa Rica
34-10-48

The Victoria Trust
P.O. Box 1023
2240AB Wassenaar, Holland

United Nations Environmental
   Program
United Nations Plaza
New York, NY 10017

Whole Earth Satellite Network
13445 Ventura Blvd.
Sherman Oaks, CA 91413
(818) 829-4736

World Citizens Assembly
25 Anchos Vista, #26
San Anselmo, CA 94960
(415) 457-0633

World Peace Center
P.O. Box 95062
Lincoln, NE 68509
(402) 477-4733

About the Author

Gabriel Cousens, M.D., is a holistic physician, psychiatrist, homeopath, family therapist, certified Essene minister, Reiki master, meditation teacher since 1973, codirector of the first kundalini clinic in the U.S., and the author of *Spiritual Nutrition and the Rainbow Diet,* which was called by *Meditation Magazine* "the best book on diet from both a health and spiritual point of view ever to see print."

Dr. Cousens is currently the director of Tree of Life Seminars, which offers four workshops: spiritual nutrition, spiritual fasting, Reiki, and the Zero Point Process (how to create peace with the mind). These seminars are designed to give people a direct understanding of the Sevenfold Peace and the fourteen Essene Communions with the Earthly Mother and Heavenly Father. Dr. Cousens has presented these seminars throughout the United States, Canada, and Western and Eastern Europe.

Since 1963, Dr. Cousens has been involved in efforts to create peace in the world. These efforts have included working with black teen gangs on the Southside of Chicago; establishing a teen center for white working-class teens in Boston; developing a nationally funded school health program in the Central Harlem schools; cofounding the Petaluma People's Service Center, which has been actively serving the people of Petaluma since 1975; and antiwar organizing. He has also served as the chief mental health consultant for Operation Headstart in Sonoma County. Since 1985, Dr. Cousens has worked as the founder and director of Sonoma County Peace the 21st, an international thought form for peace movement. He is also on the board of directors of the National Coalition to Stop Food Irradiation, and on the Circle of Advisors of the Global Family.

Dr. Cousens graduated from Amherst College and received his medical degree from Columbia Medical School. He was associated with the National Institute for Mental Health for three years. He has published articles in the fields of biochemistry, school health, clinical pharmacology, hypoglycemia, and Alzheimer's disease. He is listed in *Who's Who in California*. He has been happily married since 1967 and has two children, seventeen and twenty years old.

Dr. Cousens is currently completing two additional books to be published by H J Kramer Inc: *Tao of Nutrition* and *Joyful Survival in the 1990s*.

For information on Dr. Cousens's Tree of Life Seminars or Peace the 21st, call (707) 778-6501, or write to Gabriel Cousens, M.D., 200 Spring Hill Rd., Petaluma, CA 94952.

BOOKS THAT TRANSFORM LIVES
FROM H J KRAMER INC

WAY OF THE PEACEFUL WARRIOR
by Dan Millman
A tale of transformation and adventure . . . a worldwide best-seller.

TALKING WITH NATURE
by Michael J. Roads
"From Australia comes a major new writer . . . a magnificent book!"
—RICHARD BACH, Author, *Jonathan Livingston Seagull*

THE EARTH LIFE SERIES
by Sanaya Roman, Channel for Orin
A course in learning to live with with joy,
sense energy, and grow spiritually.

LIVING WITH JOY, BOOK I
"I like this book because it describes the way I feel
about so many things."—VIRGINIA SATIR

PERSONAL POWER THROUGH AWARENESS:
A GUIDEBOOK FOR SENSITIVE PEOPLE, BOOK II
"Every sentence contains a pearl . . ."—LILIAS FOLAN

SPIRITUAL GROWTH:
BEING YOUR HIGHER SELF, BOOK III
Orin teaches how to reach upward to align with the
higher energies of the universe, look inward to expand
awareness, and move outward in world service.

AMAZING GRAINS: CREATING VEGETARIAN MAIN
DISHES WITH WHOLE GRAINS
Amazing Grains makes the process of learning and cooking
into what it is meant to be—a joy." —JOHN ROBBINS,
Author, *Diet for a New America*

MESSENGERS OF LIGHT: THE ANGELS'
GUIDE TO SPIRITUAL GROWTH
by Terry Lynn Taylor
At last, a practical way to connect with the angels
and to bring heaven into your life!

JOURNEY INTO NATURE: A SPIRITUAL ADVENTURE
by Michael J. Roads
An unforgettable book about humanity as
perceived through the eyes of nature.